GLIMPSES of HEAVEN(er)

GLIMPSES of HEAVEN(er)

PAT LINVILLE BURROUGHS

Deeds Publishing | Athens

Published by Deeds Publishing in Athens, GA
www.deedspublishing.com

Printed in The United States of America

Cover design by Mark Babcock.

ISBN 978-1-950794-40-9

Books are available in quantity for promotional or premium use. For information, email info@deedspublishing.com.

First Edition, 2021

10 9 8 7 6 5 4 3 2 1

So many people are responsible for this book happening and I wish I could personally have thanked each one of you, or at least mentioned your name in this book. Throughout my life, so many in HEAVENer have brightened my life and lifted my spirits. Without the help of my Heavenly Father, nothing good would have come to me. Family members, too many to name, have given me a good life—and lots of stories to share with others. Many people have encouraged me in my writing addiction, and without them this book, humble though it may be, would never have happened. My husband and our kids, Sandy and Jim, have shown me more love and patience than I could ever have believed would be mine if I lived a hundred years. I dedicate this book to each and every one of you. If your name doesn't appear on this page, please chalk it up to a bit of senility on my part. You are loved and appreciated. Thank you all so much.

Contents

Preface

As fifth graders, my classmate, Alton Manifold and I used to write stories for each other. He was very witty and I loved reading his funny stories. He also had a great laugh and I loved to hear it, especially when he was laughing at me. So we wrote stories we thought the others would enjoy. I don't remember if anyone else ever read them, but the two of us enjoyed writing them.

In high school English classes, I always enjoyed writing assignments. As I recall, I never had any aspirations to become a famous writer, not because I thought I did or did not have what it would take to be one. I just liked to write, in the same way that I like to eat, read, or be with my family. And I had no need or desire for fame.

I married right after high school graduation. The Lord just put the man in my life that He meant for me to have and it didn't matter to either of us that we had absolutely nothing needed to set up housekeeping. But that's another story and I won't go into it now. I attended some college later on but never found time to graduate.

My friend Alton went off to work on a big-city newspaper, where to the best of my knowledge, he worked basically all of his adult life. I'm sorry to say he didn't live to be old. He and his sweet wife, Eva, both died quite young and are buried in the cemetery north of our town.

From time to time I wrote something when inspired to do so, including letters to the editor in various newspapers and was even published in Home Life magazine a few times as well as a time or two in Mature Living. I especially enjoyed writing for Associated Content, Heavener Online, and I still get much enjoyment from writing with my Facebook friends.

Through the years, people have been very kind to me regarding my writing. Many have said, "You need to write a book." I never really considered actually doing that until recently when it seemed the circumstances just fell into place and the right people came into my life with encouragement and offers of help that I found hard to refuse. My publisher/editor, Bob Babcock of Deeds Publishing has literally made it possible for me to publish this book and has encouraged me every step of the way.

Craig Hall, owner and editor of The Heavener Ledger has been a great source of encouragement to me for many years, and I appreciate him so much. More people than I can name have brightened my days with words of encouragement through the years. May God bless you richly for your kindness! Through the years I have saved computer files of incidents and blurbs I have written for various entities. This book contains many of these incidents which can be read individually as desired. I hope the readers can find some enjoyment in them. I apologize for using so many personal and family references, but since I'm writing this book mainly for my family, I feel I should mention them here and there.

Love Letter to Jesus

Back in the 1990's when I was secretary at First Baptist Church in Heavener, Oklahoma, I went to the Post Office to pick up the church mail one day and found a strange letter in our box. It was addressed to: "Jesus in Heaven," written in a child's penmanship and obviously doctored up some by an employee in a post office in upstate New York, where the letter was postmarked. Someone had apparently looked in a directory and found a town with a name as near to "Heaven" as possible. They had added "er" to the "Heaven" and "OK" after that. And it reached the Post Office in our town. Heavener is a very small town and things work here that wouldn't work in a big city. I never knew for sure, but assumed that because the people in the local post office knew my husband had worked for the post office for 35 years, and that I worked for a local church, they thought I might come as close as anyone to getting the letter into the hands of someone who would know what to do with it.

I opened the letter and read, "Dear Jesus, I love you. " It was signed "Angelia." Someone had apparently put her return address on the envelope before putting it in the mail.

I hated to think of a child being disappointed, but wasn't quite sure how to handle the situation. I finally decided to write her a letter on church letterhead stationery and tell her that since I was Jesus' secretary, I would answer her letter for Him. I didn't feel that was stretching the truth too far. I mailed it to the return address on her letter and was surprised to soon receive another letter from her, addressed to me. I don't remember what I told her, other than that Jesus was happy to know she loved Him and that He loved her so much as well. Through the next few years, we occasionally sent letters back and forth, but as she was growing up, her letters came less and less often and finally stopped altogether.

Early in our correspondence, I received a letter from her grandmother thanking me for answering the little girl's mail, because she had written such letters several times before and never received a reply. It's not likely that I'll ever hear from her again, but I'm glad I had the chance to know her for a while. That was one of the advantages of living in HEAVENer.

Where is Heavener?

The little town of Heavener sits nestled in the mountains of eastern Oklahoma, ten miles from the Arkansas line. It's easy to drive through it on Highway 59 and never really notice it unless you're looking for the Heavener Runestone or a bite to eat. The KCS (Kansas City Southern) railroad runs right through the middle of Heavener. Highway 59 runs down the west side of the railroad tracks and the downtown area is on the other side. There are three crossings in about a mile and another one a mile or so farther north. Probably the biggest complaint about the railroad has been that it doesn't matter how many times you need to cross the tracks in a day, chances are great that you're going to have to wait on a train, or attempt to find a crossing that's open, which can really eat up the time. And it has always been that way.

Wikipedia has some interesting facts about Heavener regarding its name and establishment as a town. *"Joseph H. Heavener and some other white settlers arrived, secured permits to farm from the Choctaw Indians and settled down to farm. In 1880, Zachary Taylor Ward and his Choctaw Indian wife, Tabitha Hickman Ward, moved their store at Skullyville to the present site of Heavener. Ward died in 1883, and his widow, Tabitha, married Heavener. The couple owned the land on which the town was established. Prior to being named Heavener by a popular vote in 1895, the area was known by several different names, including Prairie of the Tall Grass, Choctaw City, Prairie View, Long Prairie, and Grand Prairie.*[3]

At the time of its founding, and through Oklahoma's entry into statehood in 1907, Heavener was located in Sugar Loaf County, one of the counties making up the Moshulatubbee District of the Choctaw Nation. "

I found the information in Wikipedia to be very interesting. There's more than I could include here, but to anyone interested, it's worth looking up.

The Heavener Runestone

Heavener's one claim to fame at this time is the Heavener Runestone, which is on the hill (known as Poteau Mountain) on the east edge of town. When I was growing up, from the age of about seven, we climbed that mountain a few times just because we could, without knowing the Runestone was a literal stone's throw away. After I married, we heard about the stone, and drove a mile or so north on Morris Creek Road to Benson Lane and from there walked up a canyon that led back to the Runestone. The Runestone, which is a huge vertical slab of rock, at some time in the distant past apparently fell from the cliff above and stuck up in the ground below, making an excellent place for someone to carve strange characters on the stone. For years it was the subject of many studies regarding the person who carved the figures on it. A few decades ago, the consensus was that it was done by Viking explorers to the region, who apparently had traveled up the Arkansas River and then smaller tributaries to reach the area.

But Wikipedia now indicates that that might not be totally accurate either. Quoting Wikipedia, "***Heavener Runestone Park** is a 55-acre (220,000 m²) park located in Le Flore County, Oklahoma. It* *is located near the city of Heavener, Oklahoma.*[1] *Formerly a state park of Oklahoma, it was transferred to the City of Heavener in 2011, and is now operated by the Friends of Heavener Runestone, a non-profit organization. The Viking Festival held at the park on two weekends a year serves as a fundraiser for operating and maintaining the park."*

Opened in 1970, the park has been erected around the Heavener Runestone, a runestone found in 1923, and most likely inscribed in the 19th century, perhaps by a Swedish immigrant. The stone is located on Poteau Mountain just outside the town's limits."

Heavener resident Gloria Farley spent many years researching the Runestone and finally succeeded in getting it recognized. She was largely responsible for it becoming well-known nationwide and for the eventual construction of the Runestone State Park.

For more information, see https://www.okhistory.org/publications/enc/entry.php?entry=HE007

The way most of us around here see it, we may never know for sure who carved the characters on the stone. To us, it doesn't really matter. We just love the stone, the peaceful valley that shelters it, the waterfall that keeps the area cool in the summer, and the beautiful park built to celebrate its presence.

Runestone Park is a lovely place on the mountain, with steps leading down from the parking area to the Runestone, which years ago was encased in a small building with a glassed-in area to protect the stone from the elements and from vandals. The park is a peaceful respite from the rest of the world, and we are blest to be able to drive to it from our home in five minutes or so (providing we can get across the railroad tracks.) There are a number of picnic shelters, two larger outdoor shelters and a large building which can be rented to accommodate a sizeable number of people for parties and other social functions, and even an amphitheater. There are also a gift shop, playground equipment, and good walking trails. But mostly it's a quiet place near home where a family can go enjoy a picnic and just relax. There is no admission fee to the park and all are welcome.

Our Early Years in Heavener

My family moved to Heavener in April of 1941, from Forester, AR, my birthplace, when I was about a month old. My dad, Earl Linville, went to work with his brother, Carl, in a metal shop building almost next door to Dunn's grocery on the south end of Main Street. We moved into an old house that was just a little south of the shop. It sat almost in the street, with only a sidewalk separating the front door from the traffic. One of the very few pictures taken of me as a baby was one with Mother standing on the sidewalk in front of that old house, beside a big black baby buggy with a bald-headed baby in it.

With the exception of a couple of times when we moved back to Arkansas for a very brief period, Heavener has been my home all my life. I saw Heavener at its best and brightest, and now I'm seeing it suffer and fade away like so many other small towns. The nice houses in town are mostly gone now, or unrecognizable. Most people who choose to build a new house here are going outside the city limits. We did the same. But it's still Heavener and it's still home. It has been a good place to live.

We used to have many stores, including several grocery stores, a Ben Franklin store, and later a variety store that took its place, Stringer's five and ten, three drug stores, a couple of hardware stores, five dry goods stores, two or three furniture stores, numerous gas stations, a bakery, a movie theater, several new car dealerships, and several doctors. We now have basically the bare essentials. Heavener now has one dry goods store, Bernard's, which sells mostly western wear. The doctors have been replaced by two PA's. There was even a small hospital at the time my little brother, my eldest nephew and niece were born in the early 50's. Now the nearest hospital of any kind is at Poteau, 14 miles away, but at least the road between Heavener and Poteau is much better than it was back then so the trip seems much shorter now.

Currently, we have one grocery store, CV's, with a very good stock of all kinds of groceries and a good bakery, as well as a food bar with good food ready to take home and enjoy. There are also several smaller Mexican food stores, two excellent Mexican restaurants, El Celaya, and La Magia, which serves not only good Mexican food, but has a wonderful offering of goodies baked on site. There are also several smaller Mexican food places that serve a good taco, etc, a Simple Simon's pizza place, and the Southern Belle restaurant, which is in an authentic KCS railroad dining car. Dollar General and The Family Dollar, which serve as good replacements for many of the stores that are now gone, sell a sizable stock of groceries as well as some clothing and a little of everything. Three service stations also sell a few grocery items. Having become used to the convenience of Walmart, we sometimes feel a bit deprived here, but I remember so many years when we actually had fewer resources here in town than we do now. I do miss all the stores that were downtown and the people who worked in them, but I suppose that's the price we have to pay for "progress."

Our children grew up in Heavener, as I did. My husband, Clem

Lee Burroughs, was born and raised at Howe, about five miles north of Heavener. I realize that proper grammar dictates the use of "reared" as opposed to "raised." But we weren't reared. We were raised. Here we later nursed our parents and several siblings through their final years. That phase of our lives is over now, as our parents passed away decades ago, we lost my last surviving sibling on Pearl Harbor Day in 2019, and my husband's siblings have all been gone for several years.

The first year we were married, my husband worked in Henry Moore's grocery store and mowed about 30 lawns all summer while working part-time for the Post Office. Then he was a regular Heavener city letter carrier for 35 years before retiring and going to work 10 months later for the school system as assistant technology director, where he stayed for 14 years. He thoroughly enjoyed that job and made many friends there. He retired at the age of 70, with thoughts of getting in some travel, but other than the wonderful trip we made to England to visit his nephew who teaches school on an air base there, we've done very little traveling since he retired.

Clem's Parents

Clem was "the child of their old age" to his parents. His dad was 55 and his mother 43 when he was born. She told one of his older sisters, when she asked why they would want another child at that age, that she wanted someone to take care of her in her old age. I'm sure she thought she would outlive her husband and be left alone. But she passed away six weeks before he did. My husband and I took care of both of them till they passed away in 1973.

My father-in-law, Alfred Burroughs, was one of the kindest, sweetest men I've ever known. I can't see him ever doing anything to hurt another person unless he was forced to, but he was also strong and hard as nails, and not someone you'd want to try to push too far. I can't believe he ever bothered anyone in his whole life, but at the same time, he knew how to stand up for himself when necessary.

His mother died when he was about 18 months old, and his father didn't remarry till he was five. The girl his father married was only fifteen at the time, but she was a good mother to the little boy as he grew up. And in return, he was the one who took care of her in her last years.

When he was in his early 30's, he went to Galveston to help in disaster recovery after a terrible hurricane hit there. He later said he was very lonely after that and started giving some thought to marriage. From things he said years later, we believe he had had a girl friend who lived in Arkansas, Elsie Hopper, whom he would have married, but she died young. When he returned to Arkansas after the work in Galveston, he married Mathey Larimore when he was 33 and she was 21. My husband was the last of their five children, and he was born after most of the others were fully grown. His nearest sibling was nine years old when he was born.

Pap, as we all called him, worked his small acreage in Howe, OK for years, and worked at many other things as well, including going to California to work for DiGeorgio Ranch when Clem was in the first grade. They stayed out there a year or two and moved back to Howe.

Pap walked about eight miles each way five days a week to help build Wister Dam back in the late 40's and early 50's. During that time he took Clem to the dam to go fishing. Clem was about 10 and always in pretty good shape, but he said that walk just about killed him. The old man was tough and wiry and never gained any weight, no matter what. He could walk forever, even when he was very old.

While living in Howe, the family had no vehicle till Clem was old enough to drive, and his older brother, George, bought him an old car to have to take their parents to the doctor and wherever they needed to go. Pap used an old homemade hand cart to transport their milk cans to the train to ship to market and to carry cattle and chicken feed home when he bought it from the little store in downtown Howe. Several different people who had lived at Howe back then told us of an incident that had happened back in the 1940's. One day when the streets were muddy and he could barely push the old cart, he gave up and moved the cart up onto the wooden sidewalk. Some man who was called a "constable" or some such, chewed him out unmercifully and ordered him off the sidewalk. As was his nature, he didn't say a word, but just did as told. However, a few minutes later he was back with his cart, with a shotgun laid across it. We were told he completed his mission and took his feed home with no further interference and without speaking a word.

Years later, when he was living in his little house between ours and the railroad, some rough guys, probably drunk, came from the nearby railroad to his open window that faced out on the dirt road to the railroad, and started harassing him. He just calmly walked across his one room and started loading his old shotgun. One of the guys yelled at him, "Hey old man! Are you going to call the police?"

He quietly said, "No, I'm not going to call the police," and approached the window with the shotgun. His tormentors left in a hurry and didn't return.

He was a wonderful dad and grandpa and our kids loved him dearly. He was barely taller than I was, so our little son called him "Wo Pap" (Low Pap) and my dad who was taller "High Pap". I can remember taking my daughter, who was less than two at the time, out to his house and asking him to watch her till I could make a quick trip to the grocery store. We had only one vehicle at the time and Clem drove it to work, so I had to walk that day. And it was cold! When I left, Pap was sitting in his rocking chair with her on his lap in her little red coat enjoying being rocked. When I returned, she was on his bed, sleeping peacefully, still in her little red coat. That's a picture that has stayed with me all these years.

When she was about four, he built her a little house in our back yard, using a washing machine box he had apparently gotten from a store downtown, some wooden strips, and haywire. She loved that little house and played in it all day. That night it stormed and the little house was destroyed. She was devastated. So we immediately started the task of building her a "real" playhouse with all the right materials. It was a nice building, but she didn't seem to care for it and seldom played in it. It just wasn't the same. He also made her a rocking horse out of some kind of an old wooden block he had picked up on the railroad and shaped it with a rasp and sandpaper, and some other scraps of wood he found around his place. The saddle horn was a wooden spool. Now a grandmother many times over, she still has that wooden horse in a special room in her house.

When our son was small, Pap taught him how to do many things he had grown up doing. One thing, that I didn't particularly care for, was how to make a trap to catch birds. Looking back now, I think he may have been teaching him skills to help him survive should really hard times ever come. There may have been times in his past when that would have been a valuable thing to know. But strangely, he lived 90 years and never killed even a deer. He said he just never wanted to kill one. Knowing how much they had needed that meat at times makes me think he was just too soft hearted to kill such a beautiful animal.

We were going to church at Howe Faith Baptist back in the 1970's and Cecil McGehee was our pastor. Sometimes Pap would go with us, although by then he was so deaf he couldn't hear much that was said. But he did enjoy the music.

Towards the last of his life he had a lot of depression along with his failing health. He wanted to die but didn't know he wasn't prepared to meet the Lord.

One day I was getting ready to go to an appointment and my brother had come to pick up our kids to take them to stay with him and our parents while I was gone. As I went out to put the kids in the car, Pap came walking out and told me he needed to talk to me. I told him I'd be out there in a few minutes. Later when I started to his house, I saw him walking up the ramp at the railroad, which was built for dump trucks to back up and unload clay into a hopper car. I knew he couldn't hear me call, so ran up behind him to talk to him. It startled him and he turned around and started waving me back, telling me to go home and come back later. As he talked he was sidling towards the edge of the ramp and, fearing he was going to fall, I caught his arm. Suddenly I realized he was intending to jump off the ramp. I said, "You're not thinking about doing what I think you are, are you?"

He said, "If you couldn't sleep nights for having nightmares and didn't feel like doing any work, you'd want out of it, too, and I'm getting out!" I asked him what he thought the Lord would think about him taking his own life and he said, "I don't know. I haven't asked him." He was old and weak and I was young and strong, so I was able to hold him there till he gave up and agreed to go back to his house and not hurt himself. I walked him back to his house, but was afraid to get away from a window when I got to mine. I called and cancelled my appointment and watched his house till Clem came home for lunch.

That happened another time later when I had finally had to break down and go to buy groceries. When I got home, I found a note he had left on the gate, "I'll be out at the dump. Hope you all have a long and happy life." I immediately rushed to his house and he was fine. In fact, he barely remembered the incident. He finally said he had gone out to the dump and stayed a while, but eventually changed his mind and came home. (The dump was what he called the place the dump trucks backed up to dump the clay.)

We were concerned about him in several ways. He had told us

that when he was younger, he had chosen to go to church at the Methodist church at Cauthron because he liked the pastor better than the one at the Baptist church and those were his only two choices. He told of seeing boys who drank and the way they acted and was determined not to live his life that way. It seemed he had always tried his best to do right. But did he understand that Jesus had died for him? He used to sit out on his little porch and read the Bible a lot, but never seemed comfortable to discuss spiritual matters. Clem tried to talk to him about it, and thought he was "okay" but now there was the matter of him trying to take his own life. That was a constant concern.

When he was in the hospital the last time with heart failure, he called me on Friday and asked me to come and get him. I told him I'd talk to his doctor. We had been going to see him every night, but now he wanted to come home. I called his doctor and he said if we took him home before they could get some more of the fluid out from around his heart, he would die right away. He said we should stay away from the hospital till Monday and let them try to help him improve enough to come home.

It was so hard for us not to go see him on Saturday and especially on Sunday after church. But about 2:00 o'clock that afternoon our phone rang and it was our pastor. He had asked about going to visit him in the hospital and we had said it would do no good because Pap couldn't hear well enough to understand him and probably wouldn't remember him because his memory was just about gone. But our pastor said he had felt compelled to go see Pap, so he went. When he got to his room, Pap was crying, and his roommate was asleep.

So the pastor started talking to him—asked if he knew who he was. He said, "Yes, you're Clem and Pat's pastor." That was a surprise, partly because he understood what the pastor had asked him and partly because he recognized him.

In the course of the conversation, Bro. Cecil asked him if he had ever asked Jesus to come into his heart, forgive him of his sins, and take over his life. He said, "No, I can't say that I ever did just that." When Bro. Cecil asked him if he'd like to do that, he said he would, so Bro. Cecil prayed with him. Afterwards Pap said he was so relieved and so glad he had done that.

Our phone started ringing and rang the rest of the afternoon. One call was from one of Clem's high school classmates, Louise Searles, telling us that she had gone to the hospital to visit Pap and he was telling her what had happened. And that he was so happy.

Another was Clem's mother's sister, who had also gone to visit him and found him a changed man. He had told her his good news and rejoiced to tell it.

Still another was Atha Roberts, who had worked at the local drugstore for years. She said she had met Clem's aunt coming out of Pap's room and she told her what had happened to him, so she had to go in. She asked him if he knew her. He said, "I sure do. You're that "girl" that works in the drugstore." He told her that he had just found the Lord and said he had wasted 90 years and he asked her to pray that he could make up for all the years he had wasted.

Pap was allowed to come home the next day. But by then his mind was gone again, his hearing had failed again, and he was too weak to talk much. I believe the Lord gave him a day with a good mind, good hearing, and sent the right man to talk to him at a time when there were no interruptions. And He prepared Pap's heart to receive the Word.

Pap went home to his Lord nine days later. What a blessing to know he was ready to go!

Helping a Bit with the Income

Clem never wanted me to work outside the home as long as the kids were little, and I wasn't in favor of it, either. I wanted to raise my own kids and would have missed them horribly. And I was blessed to be able to do so. I mostly stayed home and enjoyed our little ones, and ran a home-based cake decorating business for almost twenty years, worked on renovating our old house, and did what I could to help his aging parents. My dad helped us build a cake shop out back so I had an acceptable place to bake and decorate cakes. I made all kinds of cakes, including many wedding cakes, which I always delivered and set up. It eventually became a six-days-a-week, sixteen-hours- a-day-job.

A few years after we lost Clem's parents, my parents' health was fading, requiring a lot of attention and transportation to doctors in neighboring towns. So I was staying busy.

Eventually, completely burned out from baking and decorating cakes, but mostly from cleaning up the mess I made, and with the kids out on their own, I gave that up and worked in various businesses around town. I worked in a couple of grocery stores, a "variety store," cooked in a restaurant, cleaned houses, and did just about any job that came my way. I even did a bit of dry wall finishing—by request. From time to time, I taught cake decorating classes at Carl Albert State College and in my shop at home, and also worked as a substitute teacher for a couple of years. My last job was as secretary of First Baptist Church for seven years. My favorite, though unpaid, job of all was as a tutor with first graders who needed special help. I wish I could have done that all my life. Although I've taught cake decorating classes and have taught kids to swim, there's nothing to compare to the joy of seeing the light come on for a child who has been struggling to learn to read and finally figures it out.

Loving All the Little Ones

When Hispanics started moving into Heavener to work at the chicken processing plant, we encountered many little ones who could not even speak English. I remember one little boy who was brought to enroll in one of the first grade classes while I was volunteering. At the time, I was working with a first grader in the work room across the hall from the room the little boy was to be enrolled in, and saw him standing outside that door, crying and apparently terrified. I took some "suckers" (lollipops, "palettas") from my hidden stock and went across the hall to talk to him. While I couldn't speak his language, I could give him a hug and a paletta and he cheered up some. I watched him the rest of the year but was never able to work with him because of the language barrier. At the first of the next year, I went into his room to talk to his teacher, and he came up to the desk to talk to me. He said, "Hey, I can speak English now!" And he could. I was always amazed at how quickly some of those little people learned the language and to read. Many of them are at the top of their class within a few years.

Ruby

I was told that the family of one of the little girls, Ruby, was going to have a very hard Christmas, so I dropped by their mobile home to check on them. It seemed that Ruby was the only family member who spoke English and I soon learned that she was a very resourceful little person.

Since my husband worked at the school, he was careful about doing anything that could "look bad" to the school administrators. He said he had been told not to allow students and especially little girls, to be at our house nor to give them a ride in his car. I felt and still feel that was a bit extreme, but he did try to stay within those guidelines. He was planning to buy me a new set of rings for Christmas, as the ones he bought me when we married were of necessity on the small and modest side. I never minded, but he always wanted to get better ones for me when finances allowed. I've never cared for expensive jewelry, mainly because I don't trust myself not to lose it, so I asked him if I could use part of the price of the rings to help that little family have a better Christmas. And as usual, he granted my request.

I drove back over to Ruby's house and asked her to interpret so

I could talk to her mother. She had a small brother, and in addition to her parents, an uncle was living with them. I asked her to tell her mother that I would like to take her shopping for Christmas presents for her family if that was agreeable with her. She was not as young as some of the students' parents I had met, and looked like she had probably had a hard life, but she was very sweet. So we set a time for me to come back and get her to take her shopping.

While I was getting back in my car to leave, Ruby was carrying on a hasty conversation with her mother. As I was about to pull out, she came running and got in my car, telling me that she had permission to go home with me and stay till 5:00 o'clock. My husband was still at work and I dreaded for him to come home. When he got home, he went upstairs and stayed till time for me to take Ruby home, trying to avoid any contact with Ruby that could in any way be misunderstood. And when I returned from taking her home, he again explained to me the rules he was supposed to abide by. There was nothing I could do about it.

When the agreed-upon time came, I went and picked up Ruby's mother, who, of course, brought along the little brother. He was a very good little guy who caused no problems at all. Since Heavener had only a Dollar General at the time as a resource to buy anything for Christmas, we went there. Her mom started out by picking out the smallest, most inexpensive gifts she could find. I did persuade her to pick out a nice gift for the little boy and had Ruby show us something she would like. I would buy it later so she couldn't know for sure what she was getting. I don't remember what Catalina bought for her husband, probably socks, and when I mentioned the uncle, she picked up one pair of socks. I indicated that she should pick out something more substantial for both men and she kept saying, "Too mas, too mas." (Too much.) We finally wound up the shopping trip with my wallet not much lighter, but it was the best I could do. I learned that those people enjoy giving as much as anyone and never want to feel like a burden.

A few days after the shopping trip, we were in our upstairs apartment, where we used to stay in cold weather, as it took less gas to heat it than to heat the whole house. It had actually snowed a little and we heard tires crunching in the snow, looked out the window, and saw Ruby's family exiting the car in our driveway and heading for our house. They came in with gifts for us. I suspected that those things had been given to them and felt really bad to take them. But it seemed important to them. Ruby immediately asked to take her parents downstairs to see the rest of the house. I felt really bad for her because the mobile home they were living in was in such a sad condition. Most houses would be like mansions in comparison.

One day a little later on, I dropped by their house for some reason, and Ruby's mom was cooking their supper. Ruby had not yet made it home from school. Of course Catalina wanted to feed me and while I hated to eat their food, I also didn't want to hurt her feelings. She gave me a tortilla with a little mound of something that looked like chocolate pudding beside it and motioned for me to eat it. I postponed it as long as I could, and finally Ruby arrived home from school. She insisted that I eat it and I asked what the brown stuff was. Was it chocolate pudding? I wasn't sure when or how to eat what. Ruby had a good laugh and told me it was mole (molay) which I recognized as a Mexican food I had heard of before.

Having been in the business for many years, I baked and decorated a cake for Catalina when her birthday came. Not a big deal for me. But when my birthday rolled around, they went to the local Mexican bakery and had a special cake made for me. I knew it had to be a financial hardship on them and told myself I would just have to not do anything for them in the future that might cause them to feel a need to reciprocate.

I enjoyed that sweet family for a few months, then one day Ruby failed to show up at school and I asked one of her friends if she knew if Ruby was sick. She said no, that they had moved back to Mexico. Just like that. Here today, gone tomorrow. The only thing I ever heard about the family after that was when Ruby's little friend told me that Ruby's mother had died. From what she said, the best she could explain, I gathered that her mother had been expecting another baby, sat down on a chair which collapsed with her, and she hemorrhaged to death.

That trashy old trailer is still sitting empty over there across town, literally falling apart. No one has lived there for years. I feel like crying every time I drive by it.

Emelio

I worked with one tiny boy, Emilio, who looked to actually be about four, after his teacher asked me to take him out and find out how much English he spoke. He was very quiet and seldom said much of anything. But once alone with him, I found out right away that he spoke excellent English and knew a little bit about everything. It was obvious that he watched a lot of TV. His teacher said that he had been sent to kindergarten in another state, then during the year the family had moved to Heavener (the year before), and they had enrolled him in the first grade, but he had soon been put back in kindergarten. This year he had once more been enrolled in the first grade and didn't seem to have a clue about even the alphabet. But he was no dummy.

In working with him, I soon learned that he loved animals. So I bought a set of cheap plastic animals, printed the name of each animal on a sheet of paper, and set the animal above its name on the paper. When it was his turn for me to work with him, I showed him the animals and asked if he'd like to have them. Of course he said he would. So I told him that if he could read me all the letters in an animal's name, he could have that animal. He wasn't remotely interested in reading the letters, but he wanted the animals. In about a week, he owned all the animals, but he still wasn't interested in those "stupid" letters. I started working with him on the sound each letter made, and starting printing them into words and having him sound them out. Suddenly it was like the light came on. Oh, so that's what these letters are all about! And soon he was reading.

One day I noticed that Emilio was not at school and wondered if he was sick. Then someone came to the room I was in and told me he had had a terrible accident and was in the hospital. No one was really sure exactly what had happened, but years later he told me all about it. I'm sure his family knew, but tried to keep it quiet. He had a mentally challenged uncle who lived with them. He told me that he and some other kids were playing hide-and-seek and he got the idea to climb up the ladder where his uncle was working on the roof of an old storage building, and hide up there. His uncle had seen him coming and laid a section of shingles over a large hole he had made in the roof. Emilio had crawled up on the shingles and had fallen through the roof, breaking the ball off the ball-and-socket joint on his hip.

He was taken to the children's hospital in Little Rock, AR, where he had surgery and was put in a cast. I went to his house and worked with him on reading and later one of the teachers went over and worked with him some on other subjects. When he came back to school, we were a matched set. I was having major problems with my left hip by then and when we walked down the hall together to go to the library, both limping, we must have been an interesting sight. Emilio later wound up in a body cast in an effort to help him walk straighter, and when it was removed, he even had a little walker, a miniature of the one I used after I had my hip replaced. He eventually recovered enough to walk with barely a limp and the last time I saw him he said that he has no pain in his hip.

As soon as he was able to get out after his surgery, I started bringing him to our house (regardless of policy, and no one said a negative word about it) and when he had recovered enough, I would put him in our hot tub to exercise his leg. When the weather warmed up, I took him to our next-door neighbor, Betty's house to swim in her pool. He learned to swim in about an hour's time and before long was swimming the length of her pool. He was like a grandchild to Clem and me for a number of years. His family moved to Arkansas and back and after they moved back, we saw little of him. The last time we saw him, he came to our house selling vacuum cleaners. He did a good job. While here he told us he had been reading a lot of books and trying to learn the proper way to do things.

When he had been in the first grade, his teacher had told me that when the kids exchanged Christmas gifts, he told the one whose gift he had received in no uncertain terms what he thought of it—and it wasn't complimentary. So later I asked him what he would do if someone gave him a gift and he didn't like it. He said, "I guess I'd just tell them I didn't like it." I went on to explain to him that it might hurt the other person's feelings if he did that, and told him he should just tell them "Thank you" as nicely as possible, and then if he didn't like the gift, give it away later. He seemed shocked about the whole concept. But he did seem to be working on learning a better way to do things. I was pleased that he was trying so hard. We haven't seen him in a few years and I'm not sure he's even still in town. We pass their house but can never tell if anyone is there. But we'll never forget him. I hope he'll still pop up at our door one of these days.

There were several of the little ones I worked with who are still around, all grown up now, but still sweet. I wouldn't take anything for the time I got to spend with them.

Early years on East First Street

During a few of my earliest years, we lived on East First Street in Heavener, after Uncle Carl closed his shop and moved to Texas. Daddy, at the time of the following incident, worked at a blacksmith shop/auto repair business two blocks from our house. The shop was at the very end of South Main St. on a corner and there was a large vacant lot between it and the nearest businesses to the north. The "county building" (LeFlore County road maintenance office) now sits just a few feet north of where this shop was located back then. It was owned by Mr. Melvin Davis who even then was getting on in years. Mr. Davis had two grandsons, Jack and Jim, who were sons of his son, Owen, and his wife, Deborah. Jack made a name for himself coaching football, in California as I recall, and Jim was an impressive pilot in the U.S. Marine Corps.

The building itself, with a dirt floor, was ancient, made of wide weathered boards, no insulation, and two big doors that swung out and had to be propped back if you wanted to leave them open. There was a forge and anvil in there and during the time he worked there, Daddy became a pretty good blacksmith. Years later, when he had his own shop, he had a forge installed and people soon learned that he could do just about any job they needed done.

When he started in his mechanic career, after years of farming and cutting logs, vehicles were so much simpler than they are today. He could fix just about anything, and often could tell what the problem with one was just by listening to it. By the time he had to retire at the age of 55, due to crippling rheumatoid arthritis, things were beginning to change in the manufacturing of vehicles, so within a few years he would have been lost in the maze of electronics. When he was put on steroids that eased his pain, he started to work on lawn mowers at home and later he said he actually made more on them than he had made on repairing cars and log trucks. He didn't believe in "robbing people" and charged such reasonable fees that people often paid him more than he asked.

My Hero, My Dad

Daddy lost his dad when he was four years old and his life had been incredibly hard after that. His mother tried to feed them but had no skills to make money so life was a struggle every day. His brother, Carl, was five years older than Daddy and between them, they tried to provide enough food for them all. Daddy was put in the cotton patch to work at the age of four. At 13, he was cooking for a road construction crew. He said he was able to attend school only part of one year, but apparently he took advantage of that year. He loved to read, had beautiful penmanship, and could figure math problems faster than some could do these days with a calculator. He had what my husband called a "gift for problem solving," and could fix anything. He was a pretty good carpenter, as well as a self-taught mechanic. He had wanted to be a doctor, but never had the opportunity to do so.

Strangely, my father-in-law had also wanted to be a doctor and almost got a chance to do it. Back then, in the early 1900's, a person could go on rounds with a doctor, I suppose what they would call "shadowing" now, learn what he could from the doctor, and eventually go out on his own. Mr. Burroughs (Pap) was planning to join a local doctor and thus start working on his education, when his dad had an accident and broke his arm. So Pap had to stay home and bring in the crops for his dad, and by the time that was done, he had lost his opportunity. I think both of our dads grieved for what might have been.

My dad, I think, considered himself a bit of a doctor all his life, anyway. We once had a hen whose craw was stopped up and her front was hugely enlarged. Daddy took a razor blade and cut her open, removed the blockage, and sewed her back up. She healed with no problems and was a family pet from then on.

For as long as he could hobble around enough to get to a neighbor's house, every morning Daddy checked on all his neighbors that he considered in worse shape than he was in. His theory on life was that, "I reckon the Good Lord put us here to help one another," and that's the way he lived his life. My mother was the same way. When Daddy was in the nursing home a few months before he died, I was surprised one day when I went up there to find two local ladies visiting him. He didn't know them well, I'm sure, but they had come to see him. Later one of them told me that when her husband was confined to the house his last few months, Daddy drove across town every Sunday to see about him. Daddy's vision was so bad he shouldn't have been driving, but he felt a need to see about this man. The man's wife wanted him to know his visits were appreciated.

We Saw a Dead Man!

One day while Daddy was working in Mr. Davis' shop, my next-older sister, Inella, and I were sent to the grocery store to pick up a few groceries. We went by the shop to get money from Daddy, then cut across the vacant lot on our way to the store another block away. We were running as kids tend to do, when one of us almost tripped over a man's body stretched across the trail. Naturally we ran back to the shop screaming, "A dead man! A dead man!" Daddy went out to investigate and found the town drunk sleeping off his overindulgence of the night before. While it probably wouldn't have been a big deal to adults to see something like that, the incident stayed with us forever.

My Brother's Mishaps in Daddy's Shop

A year or two later, Daddy built his own shop behind our house on East First Street. The last time I looked, the concrete floor was still there, all that was left of it, except for memories. The house has also been gone for years.

From the start, my older brother, Veachel spent many hours helping Daddy in the shop. I guess things mechanical were just in his blood. One day when he was helping out, some neighborhood boys came by and were hanging around with him in the shop. One of them innocently picked up a hot welding rod and stuck it in a pan of gasoline. Veachel was standing near the pan and the explosion burned him badly. It took a while for him to recover from the burns, but apparently not as long as it took the boy responsible for it. Ever since that incident, virtually every time I've run into that boy, who is now a man in his late 80's, he says, "I'll bet Veachel still hates me for that." And I tell him that Veachel never hated him or had any bad feelings towards him because he knew he would never have done it intentionally.

Veachel had more than one bad experience in that shop. I remember a time when he seemed to spend a lot of time sitting around, usually out in the swing on the front porch. At the time I didn't realize why. He told me in later years that he had been working under "one of those big old heavy cars they used to have" and the jack holding it up either broke or fell, and the car fell on him, pinning him to the floor by his hips since he had been on his side when it fell. He said that Daddy asked him if he could pull himself out if he could raise the car and he said he'd try. He said, "Daddy lifted that big old car, by himself, without using a jack or anything, and I was able to pull myself out." Daddy was not an overly big man but was strong and I guess at the moment a huge amount of adrenaline was pumping through his veins. Veachel told me that there was not a spot on his body below the waist that wasn't bruised, and it was a long time before he could do more than barely walk around. I remembered when he was hurt, but was too young at the time to realize just how badly he was injured.

Mother's Nightmare

In 1947, Mother got up one morning and said she had had the strangest dream. In her dream, she had felt a violent electric shock. And she had no idea why she would dream something like that. Later in the day someone came and told Daddy that his brother, Carl, had been killed in an accident in Texas. Back then it could take hours to make a long distance call, with the local operator calling another operator down the line, and she in turn would call another operator farther on. During the day, people were speculating on what could have happened to Uncle Carl. Mother repeatedly told them that he had been electrocuted. I'm sure people wondered about her sanity. Late in the day, word came that he had been under a car in the shop where he worked in Texas, using an electric impact wrench and at some point had laid it down on his chest to free up his hands. Unfortunately, it had rained the night before, there was a broken window in the shop, which resulted in a puddle, and when he laid the electric tool down on his chest he got his feet in the puddle. He died instantly, at the age of 42. At his funeral was the first time I had ever seen my dad cry. They brought Uncle Carl back to Muse to bury him among many of his family from generations back. From visiting the cemetery, it appears that many of his male relatives had died young. There are a lot of Linville and Simmons relatives buried there now, including Uncle Carl's wife, Elsie, and his daughter, Delmon, both of whom died young with cancer.

When Electricity Came to Town

Reliving that incident brought to mind a story my husband told this past weekend. He told about when his family first had electricity put in their house in Howe back in the '40's or '50's. Prior to that, the only light they had was from a kerosene lamp and he remembered what a pain it was to get it lit and how hard it was to see with the dim light it put out. I can relate to the problem with lighting it, because we have a couple of kerosene lamps that belonged to our folks. Years ago when we had a power outage, we attempted to light one of them. Clem set it on the hearth and tried to light it and it caught on fire. We were thankful it was on the hearth instead of on a table. I think that was the last time we ever tried to light one.

Clem talked about how bright the electric light seemed and how thankful they were to have it. Somewhere in the conversation, I asked him about receptacles—how many they had and where they were located. He said there were no receptacles at all. I thought that was so strange! Why have electricity if you have no receptacles? He went on to explain that they didn't need them because they had nothing to plug into them, and they had nothing to plug in because they had no receptacles. I guess we just can't imagine what life was like before we came along! When I was very young, some people used to have a brown electric cord hanging from the ceiling with a socket attached to it, a receptacle on each side of the socket, and a light bulb screwed into the bottom of that socket. It seemed I could remember seeing someone plug an iron into it. I suppose that was the first version of a receptacle.

I remember when we also had no electricity and no indoor plumbing, unless it might have been a faucet in the kitchen. Mother did her laundry out in the yard, heating water in an old black wash pot and scrubbing the clothes on a rub board, rinsing them in two washtubs set up on a stand Daddy had welded together, and then hanging them on lines to dry. I also remember the day the truck drove into our yard and unloaded her first washing machine. She was so happy and I know it made her life much easier.

Not long after that, Daddy added a room onto our house and put in our first indoor bathroom. That was a happy day for us all. I so hated having to go to the outhouse before then. I remember one time when we were about to drive to Arkansas to visit relatives, Daddy walked me out to the outhouse and told me to go in and "make a creek." When you had to go out in the cold and rain to take care of a necessary chore, it really became unpleasant.

I do recall, though, when we visited my uncle's family in Arkansas, my cousin and I used to visit the two-holer together and have a good visit while we did our thing.

I can also vaguely remember how Mother would heat water on her gas cook stove in the kitchen and pour it into a big washtub behind the stove. I don't remember actually being in that tub, but apparently I avoided contact with it as much as possible. I have to think it was not the water I disliked, but the embarrassment of being stripped off and plunked in that tub with family members around. I do remember one time when I saw her heating that water and knew what was about to happen, so I went off and hid. I was probably three or four at the time. I can remember seeing her come into the dimly lit bedroom where I was hiding under the bed. I watched her looking here and there, and I knew she was looking for me. Apparently I had a problem with staying focused on the subject at hand even then, as I do now. Since she was not calling my name, I soon forgot why I was under the bed and had to find out what she was up to. The next time she came into that room to look again, I was told I finally called out, "Whatcha lookin' for, Motha?" Busted!

This all reminded me of my father-in-law talking about the first automobile he had ever seen, and yet he had lived to see men walk on the moon. I find it hard to believe the next generation will see as many changes as we did and as our parents saw in their lives.

Santa's Accident

My parents never taught us to believe in Santa Claus, but Inella, in her wisdom of eight years, thought that I, as the youngest, should be taught about him. And our folks allowed it. I can remember on Christmas Eve one time when a car door slammed outside and someone said, "That must be Santa Claus! We'd better get out of sight or he won't come in and bring us anything." I'm assuming I had not been taught that Santa had a sleigh that he used on Christmas Eve. So we kids hid in our parents' bedroom and when we were called out, there were presents under the tree. That routine worked well till my sister decided I was old enough to know the truth. So she told me that Santa had been killed in a car wreck and now our parents would be providing our gifts for us. I didn't take that news too hard, since I had never met Santa personally, and as long as the gifts would keep coming anyway, it was not a big deal for a four-year-old.

Sibling Pranks and Revenge

When we were living on East First Street, one evening my parents left my two older sisters and me in the care of our older brother, Veachel, for an hour or so. He would have been about 13 or 14, Norma about 11, Inella eight, and I would have been four. He was a prankster extraordinaire, and saw this as an opportunity to get a good one on his sisters. Shortly after our parents drove away, he pulled back a kitchen window curtain and stood looking out the window for a couple of minutes. Then he yelled at us, in a state of apparent panic, "Get in the bedroom and lock the door and don't come out no matter what happens. I just saw a man go around the house with a big knife in his hand." We obediently scurried into our parents' bedroom, locked the door, and huddled, shaking with fear, as we waited to see what would happen.

Soon we heard a loud noise, such as a door being kicked in, followed by scuffling noises, a loud scream, and then… nothing. For a long time. Eventually we crept out of the bedroom and peeked into the kitchen, where we saw our brother sprawled on the floor, with blood on his neck, and a big knife on the floor beside him. He was obviously as dead as the man my sister and I had almost tripped over behind the Davis shop. It's all a blurry memory now, but I'm sure we girls all screamed and cried and ran in circles because we didn't know what else to do. He didn't let us suffer too long, though, before he jumped up, laughing his head off, and produced the catsup bottle that had held the "blood." I vowed to myself that one day I would pay him back for that, but it was a long time coming.

Fast forward a few years. In his later teens, he was girl crazy, as most boys that age are. One day he was sitting in the porch swing at our house on East Ave. B, swinging gently with a glazed look in his eyes. I was sure he was thinking about some girl, and wouldn't be paying much attention to what I was doing. So I wandered around behind the swing and pretended to be playing with something.

Earlier, I had found a strong cord about fifteen feet long and stashed it behind the swing. Now I carefully eased one end of it between the slats in the back of the swing and worked it through a protruding belt loop on the back of his jeans. It was not easy to do without his noticing, especially with the swing in motion. But I was able to do it without disturbing him, and even to tie a knot in the cord. Then, keeping plenty of slack in the cord, I tied the other end to the porch banister behind the swing. That done, I sauntered around in front of the swing, did a little dance, and sing-songed, "Nyahh nyahh nyahh nyahh nyahh—you can't catch me."

The swing was in a forward motion at the time and he bailed out of it to make a grab for me. When he hit the end of the cord, he was suspended in the air for a second, brought up short by the sudden jerk on the cord. The look on his face was priceless. Completely blank. No expression at all. Then I heard a loud snap. His belt loop had broken. It's a good thing I hadn't had the opportunity to put it through his belt, or it might have been his back that broke. But that had never occurred to me.

It took him a second to realize what had happened, then he said gruffly, "You're going to fix my belt loop!" I think now that he was trying not to laugh. He realized he had been had and was actually rather proud of my accomplishment, even if it was against him. He had taught me well. He told that story as long as he lived.

Neighbors on East First Street

I can't think about living on East First Street without thinking of the neighbors. Mr. and Mrs. Dehart lived next door to us on the south. At some point, they built a little store out front. It was very convenient for us, and I believe I was allowed to go over there every day and buy a pop and a candy bar while the others were in school. Looking back, it seems I must have been pretty spoiled, but then I don't know what special things the older ones got or were allowed to do that I didn't. I just never thought about it. The Deharts had a grandson, Barry Gilmore, who lived across town with his parents. He was a very nice boy and he had good parents. He had a beautiful collie dog that one day ran into the street to chase a motor scooter in front of the Dehart's house. He was hit by the scooter, which caused the scooter to wreck and the rider was injured. And the poor dog did not survive the accident. After we started to school, Barry was in my class for a number of years. But the Gilmores moved away before we reached High School.

When I was five, I attended a Bible School with the Hinds kids who lived across the street. They were going to the Nazarene church at the time, and they were stricter than the Baptist church

I had been used to. Doctors had just started stressing the dangers of smoking tobacco, and I understood the speaker at the Nazarene church to say smoking was a sin. My daddy had smoked since he was around 10 years old—stems and any old tobacco scraps he could get his hands on, and he rolled his own. It really tore me up to think that my Daddy was sinning by smoking, so I went straight home and talked to him about it. I know he thought he was safe in making such a deal, with my being used to getting candy and pop every day, so he said he would quit smoking if I would quit eating candy and drinking pop. I promised to do that and didn't ask for candy or pop for some time. And if he smoked I didn't know it.

After a while, I became very ill. I still can't remember ever feeling much worse than I did then. The doctor said I had malaria. Daddy came to me and said that when I got well, I could go back to the candy and pop and he still wouldn't smoke. Since then, I've wished many times that he had held me to my bargain, as it might have helped in my life-long battle with weight. He never smoked around us again, but I did catch him cheating a couple of times. When he got a little older, he realized more clearly the dangers of tobacco and did give it up completely, and said many times that he couldn't stand the smell of tobacco smoke anymore—that he thought people had to be crazy to smoke after knowing all the harm it could do a person. Mother had said that when he was smoking on a regular basis, he often had to sit up in bed to get his breath, and he would have been only in his early 30's at the time. He lived to be 87 and suffered some breathing problems in the later years, but I always felt he lived longer than he would have if he had never quit smoking all those years before.

Next door to the Hinds family, lived the Black family. The man of the family was usually known as "Bosco" or R.E, who worked for the railroad. Mrs. Black, Lessie Pearl, was one of the sweetest, kindest, most unselfish people I've ever known and my mother loved her dearly. They became very good friends and when the Blacks moved to the country, Mother was devastated. A number of years later, after we moved to Arkansas and then back to Heavener, the Blacks built a new house next door to our house on East Ave. B. Mrs. Black said she had always intended to have Mother for a neighbor again and didn't stop trying till it happened. The Blacks had two sons, Donald and Jim, and a daughter, Mary. I'm not sure what the boys did when they grew up, but Donald married our pastor's sweet daughter, Ann Vinson. Jim moved to California and we saw very little of him after that. He married a nice girl named Joyce and they had two children, a boy and a girl. I remember seeing the little girl crawling around on the floor at the age of seven months, wearing a long, full ponytail. I was so jealous of her and all that hair! I heard that Donald had passed away a few years ago, but I believe Ann is still living. I recently heard that Jim and his wife had both passed away in a very short span of time. Mary moved to the Tulsa area, married a coach, had four children, and spent over 50 years managing a "widows' colony" at Sand Springs, where women who were trying to raise children alone could live in a nice apartment for little or no rent and get a great deal of support in other ways. A few years ago I heard that she had lost one of her daughters in an accident. Mary only recently retired. I was so happy for her that she did an amazing job and helped so many people for so many years.

There was an older lady next door to the Black family when we all lived on East 1st. Mother took me over to visit her one day when I was about three years old. It seems I can remember the details clearly, but can't imagine why I would have done such a thing. Surely I knew better. But as the two of them visited, I wandered off into the kitchen and had the gall to open her refrigerator door.

Guess what was in it? Grape pop. I knew better than to ask for any, but sidled back into the living room and whined around some, like I was hungry. The poor old lady recognized the signs of hunger and asked Mother if I might want some crackers. I wanted to scream, "No, I don't want any stinkin' crackers! I want grape pop!" But somehow I knew I'd never get away with it. So we went home and Mother read me the riot act about prowling in someone else's house and asking for something. And I never did it again.

I never repeated something I had been warned about, but it seemed there were just so many things to learn and remember. One day my parents took me downtown shopping and we went to Clemo Stuart's dry goods store. It must have been close to Christmas because there were some toys there, where usually there were none. I saw a little wind-up tricycle with a Santa riding on it and it really caught my eye. Mr. Stuart told me that if I'd cry, my parents would buy it for me. So I did and they bought it. But before we got to the car I was informed that not only would that not ever work again, but there would be consequences to pay if I tried. I still have that toy, by the way, and it still works. But I don't play with it a lot these days.

Speaking of Clemo Stuart's store—it was on the ground floor of the big two-story building on the corner of Main and East Ave. D, that many remember having IOOF printed across the front of the second story. After I married, I learned that my husband's grandfather, Matthew Larimore, had once owned that building, or least he ran a hotel in it. Clem's mother had worked in the restaurant on the ground floor and was still working there when she married his dad. Their home was still at Cauthron, AR and she rode the train back and forth to work every day. Back then, the A & W (Arkansas & Western) train made several trips a day between Heavener and Waldron, AR, and Cauthron was on the way.

It must not have cost much to ride the train. Now I believe the train makes one trip a week to Waldron and back and passenger service on all trains in this area was discontinued long ago.

Many years later I worked in that building in the store Leroy and Bobbie Nolan ran for a while. Then the building was condemned because of the bad shape it was in, and they moved their store around the street to the former location of the Chevrolet dealership, which had been owned by Bill Hembree. When the dealership moved up on the highway north of town, the Appliance Center, run by Robert Holt, was opened in that building. Thankfully, somebody changed their mind and restored the IOOF building enough so it was allowed to stand, and it has had a few businesses in it since then. When Leroy and Bobbie sold the business to Brad Hill, I worked for him a while in the Appliance Center Building.

The IOOF was painted over at some point. Before that, when my kids were in grade school, they once asked me what that IOOF meant and I told them I thought it meant "International Order of Odd Fellows," who held their meetings upstairs in the building. They thought I was joking and I never did convince them I wasn't. Who would admit to being an "Odd Fellow"?

And they also didn't believe me when I told them about the song that had been around when I was in my teens about "the Purple People Eater." Thankfully it came back around for a while after that.

The Fielders

Our neighbors across the street to the north of us on East First Street were a family who had lost their husband and father in recent years, in a car accident. Irene Fielder and her three kids seemed to get along pretty well. There was Jerry, who grew up to be a well-known preacher in the Oklahoma City area. Martha Jo was a sweet little girl who grew up to marry a preacher, and Mona Gail was my age. My daddy called her Little Bear because she was so tough. She would get up on our gas meter, which was right next to the sidewalk and jump off, landing on her knees on the concrete. At the age of four. And you'd better bet she never shed a tear, either. Like me, she seemed to idolize her big brother. Although he was several years her senior, she would put on a pair of his khaki pants, cinch a belt down tight enough to keep the pants from falling off, roll up the pants legs, and she became her brother. I wondered if losing her dad had caused her to be determined to be tough, and if so, it worked. Mona Gail later became our high school girls basketball star and was also Football Queen. Irene married Aaron Roop and they seemed to be happy together as long as they lived. She got a good job at the bank and worked there for many years.

She was also the best Sunday School teacher I ever had ana ‹. sweet, generous, and charming lady.

I haven't seen any of the family in years, except at Irene's funeral a few years ago when they brought her back here for burial. I sat with Mona Gail at the graveside service and had a good visit with her. Jerry lost his beautiful daughter to cancer a number of years ago, and that's about all I know of them in recent years. They were a good family and I still miss them.

A block south of us on East First Street was a rock house where the Plummers lived. Hugh ran a grocery store and they had three kids, Doris Jean, Martha Dean, and a younger boy, Leon. The reason I remember the house is that when we would be under a tornado watch or a storm was approaching, my parents would roust us out of bed and take us down to the Plummers to wait out the storm. I never understood the necessity of doing that, but later assumed the rock house seemed more secure than the frame houses around it. I recently noticed that that rock house looks just like it did over 70 years ago. So I guess that proves it was sturdier than most of the rest of them. Martha Dean died a few years ago, and as far as I know, Doris and their brother are still living. Martha lost a son a few years before she passed away.

Across the side street from Daddy's shop, lived the Dedmon family. Henry and his wife lived in the big house, which is still where it was, and their son Dolphus and his wife Velma lived in a smaller house out back, which is long gone. Velma was a beautiful lady, somewhat younger than my mother. One day Mother was in the back yard and saw Velma come out on her front porch wearing a new dress. Jokingly, Mother whistled at her. Velma, not seeing Mother, turned and saw a man standing in front of Daddy's shop. She felt very insulted and told him about it. Mother, red-faced, had to go and apologize to both her and the man.

Mrs. Cram and her kids lived farther down the street in a house not far from the railroad at the time. Her husband had died and she was trying to raise a large family by herself. The oldest son, as I remember, was Chester, and he married my cousin, Delmon, Uncle Carl's daughter. As I recall, Dale came next. Then came Jim who grew up to become well known in Baptist circles as a musician and song-writer. When Jim had to have surgery for appendicitis as a teenager, Mother asked Mrs. Cram to let him stay with us while she was at work. She had to work to survive and was afraid to leave him alone, so he stayed with us. Neva Jane was next, and we heard after they moved away that she was severely injured in a car accident, but survived. The youngest was Stanton, known as Tinker. The only thing I remember about him was hearing that he had hitched a ride on a train from town down to where they lived. Dangerous stuff! They moved away and the last I heard were living in northwestern Arkansas. Jim died young with cancer. I haven't heard anything from that family in many years. I would love to know if any of them are still alive.

When the Carnival Came to Town

Across the street behind us was a large, vacant area where circuses and carnivals set up when they came to town. These days there is a laundromat there and Hamilton Homes is south of it. People from the carnivals would come to our house to get water, which they carried across the street to their trailers. In exchange, they gave us rolls of ride tickets. We enjoyed being the richest kids in town from time to time. But it didn't happen often enough to suit us.

I remember once when I was three or four, my parents took me to a carnival where I saw a game that had numbered squares on a floor-like area where rats were involved. Seems there were holes in the sides of a low wall around the floor and rats would run in and out of those holes. There may have been numbers over the holes in the walls that the rats ran in and out of. I don't recall exactly how the game worked, but the rules of the game aren't really that important now. This is about the rats. There was an older lady running this game, and those old brown hard-shelled bugs were flying around the bare light bulbs hanging above the game. They would fall onto the floor of the game and she would push them off with a long-handled squeegee. Later my folks let me ride the little airplane ride not far from the rat game and as the planes flew around, the bugs, attracted by all the lights, were hitting me in the face. My folks told me later that I was standing up in the plane screaming, "Help me! Stop this thing! That old rat lady is throwing bugs at me!" My parents were yelling at me to sit down and at the man running the ride to shut it down.

My Incorrigible Uncle Sherman

When I was five, we were visiting relatives in Arkansas, and my uncle Sherman was showing us his new litter of pigs. He offered to sell me the runt of the litter for a nickel. While I loved cats and dogs, I had little experience with pigs. But Sherman (named for my uncle) was a cute little rascal and I assumed would stay that way. So I went to Daddy to bum a nickel and we had a new family member. Daddy made a place for him to stay in out of the weather and started to feed him as a hog should be fed. (At first I found it hard to believe that an animal would eat "shorts" but I later developed quite a taste for them myself.)

We lived only two blocks from downtown, but that was in the 40's and farm animals in town weren't all that unusual. To my dismay, my cute little pig started growing by leaps and bounds and eventually weighed over 400 pounds. After I started to school, I came home one day to find that Sherman had become pork chops, bacon, sausage, and other equally disgusting things while I was at school. I'm sorry to say that I took it all with a grain of salt and thought no more about it. My cute little Sherman had been gone for a long time and I felt little affection for the monster who had taken his place.

Speaking of Uncle Sherman, he was a jokester and prankster unlike anyone I've met to this day. The first time my husband went with us to visit them, before we married, Uncle Sherman started in on him and kept it up the whole time we were there. One thing he said, to me, in my future husband's presence, was, "Well honey, I don't think he's so ugly," which of course was intended to indicate that I had said he was. And all during the meal he griped at Clem for eating so much. But having been forewarned, Clem would just say, "Pass some more rolls, please," or whatever. And I knew Uncle Sherman was loving it.

One thing he liked to tell about was when one of his jokes had backfired on him. He went for some of the more crude ones, and this one in particular fit that description. If someone should introduce a new wife to him, he'd say, "She's blind in one eye, and you slipped up on her blind side."

One day he was at the courthouse for some reason and a man he had known a few years earlier pointed out a woman some distance away and said, "You haven't met my wife. That's her over there."

So Uncle Sherman said, "Yeah, she's blind in one eye."

Before he could go any farther, the man said, "Yes, her first husband knocked her other eye out." Uncle Sherman still laughed when he told that, because the man had apparently been telling the truth.

When anyone went there to visit, Uncle Sherman griped constantly about how much they ate and said, "The only time I ever get anything fit to eat is when my wife's (blankety-blank) kinfolks come." Then when they were ready to leave, he loaded their car with bags of potatoes and any other kind of produce in season. He had a really big heart, but didn't want that fact spread around.

I don't claim to be psychic or anything, but I did think it was strange many years down the road when I was out in the back yard hanging clothes, and saw a denim-clad man crossing our pasture from the railroad at the back to the road out front. (Uncle Sherman always wore blue denim overalls.) I stopped to watch and he disappeared, apparently behind a cedar bush. Then he reappeared farther on, closer to the road. And then he just faded from sight again almost as if in a puff of smoke. People often cut across our pasture, but this just seemed different somehow.

I went on with my work and forgot about it for an hour or two. Then my sister called and said they had just received a call that Uncle Sherman had fallen dead of an apparent heart attack, while fighting fire in his pasture. My first thought was that even at the end he was able to take a bad situation and turn it into something dramatic.

Bicycles

My sister Inella was always a tiny little thing, and by the time she turned eight, she was still riding a 20-inch bicycle that had a "carrier" on the back. She decided when I turned four, that it was time that I learned to ride her bicycle. She would have me get in the "driver's seat" and she would sit on the back to keep the bicycle upright by putting her feet down periodically. She must have been a good teacher, because in a very short time she had me riding that bicycle up and down the sidewalk in front of our house. I never really understood why, but Veachel decided to equip me with a bicycle so Inella and I could both ride at the same time. He took the seat off his 26-inch bicycle so I could reach the pedals, although I could not sit down and ride with the seat gone. I had to put the bicycle next to the front porch and push off from the porch, and come back to the porch to get off when I was through riding.

His bicycle was very heavy and shortly after I started to ride it, I began to have a lot of pain in my neck. It became so severe that I had to stay in bed for a while. Mother was always sure the heavy bicycle was the cause of my pain, but many years later a good friend told me about something that had happened to her about the same time all those years ago when I was having the problem with my neck. She had had a "virus" or some undetermined illness, probably the same year I had my problem. Her neck was her main problem, as mine had been. Now all these years later she's having a lot of the same kind of pain I have. I have to wonder if there could be any connection between what we went through back then and the pain we have now.

After learning to ride, I had always wanted a bicycle of my own, but for some reason had never owned one of any kind. I would have been happy with a used one. So my dear brother decided to remedy that. At the time he would have been 17 or 18 and I was nine. He was working some with Daddy at the time, so had a little money to spend. On my birthday, he told me to come by the shop after school, and he would have a surprise for me. When I reached the shop, he said we were going to walk down to Otasco and get my birthday present from him. On the way, he explained to me that he had found a used bicycle down there that he was going to get me. He said it was pretty beat up, but still rideable. The word "used" didn't faze me even a little bit. I was so excited at the thought of having a bicycle of my own that I would have been happy even with a boys' junker bicycle. At that time, after a couple of family moves, I'm not sure there was a bicycle of any kind left in the family. So when we reached Otasco, I saw the most beautiful new blue and white Monarch girls' bicycle parked inside near the back. He walked over and started removing the tags from the bicycle while I stood there with my mouth open. He had pulled another prank on me, but the best one ever.

Going to Pick Wild Onions

When I started to school, I walked three blocks to the railroad, crossed the railroad, walked another block, crossed the highway, and then walked three more blocks to school. Most of the time my sister walked with me, but she was sickly and often missed school, so I sometimes had to walk it alone. One day as I stopped at a corner a block from our house, a school bus pulled up beside me and the driver opened the door and told me to get in. I saw no reason not to accept a ride on a school bus, so I climbed the steps and took a seat near the door. As soon as the door was shut, a big boy started in on me. "Do you know where we're going?" I told him I assumed we were going to school. He said, "No, we're going out to pick wild onions." I immediately started demanding to be let off the bus. Of course the driver put a stop to the harassment in a hurry, but the harm was already done.

Moving to Arkansas

In the middle of my first year in school, my folks decided to move back to Arkansas. We went to Kirby, where Mother had grown up. It was a new experience for me, because many of the people who lived there were relatives of mine, some I had already known and some who were new to me. I sometimes took girls home with me at noon to ask Mother if we were related. We lived basically next door to the school. I always thought we had a pasture behind our little barn, but realized years later it was nothing more than a large yard. But we kept a cow in it. Rather than take the long way around and walk down the highway to school, I cut across our "pasture" and crawled through a barbed wire fence to reach the school yard.

Things were really different there. One main difference was the lack of indoor plumbing, which we had had at the school in Heavener. The girl's room was behind the gym, and we had to walk down a path with smooth, round, gravel on it, down the side of the gym, to reach it. One day my cousin, Faye, who was in my class, and I asked permission to "go" during class, and were given the okay. As usual, we started off in a run, and for some reason my feet flew out from under me and I fell, face first, onto a patch of concrete that had seeped away from the rest when the gym floor was poured.

There were a number of small, pointed rocks sticking up from the surface of that concrete, and I think every one of them stuck in my face. We never even made it to the girls' room. My cousin said, "Oh, Honey!" grabbed my hand and started dragging me back to the classroom. I can still remember standing at the open door of our room, aware of the blood dripping from my face onto the wood floor. It was almost time for school to let out and for some reason my dad had come to get me. My parents took me to a doctor right away, and I suppose the doctor told them I'd probably survive. And I did. My mother thought I'd be badly scarred, but I wasn't.

I did, however, come down with scarlet fever not long after that. I was very sick for quite a while and when I finally got back on my feet, all the skin in the palms of my hands peeled off, deeply. I remember we had nice hardwood floors in the house at Kirby and we were careful not to damage them. But while I was confined with scarlet fever—after I had improved to some degree, my parents bought me a pair of rubber-wheeled skates and let me skate on those nice floors. I felt so loved.

Picking Tomatoes in Indiana

During the time we lived at Kirby—a total of 10 months—many memorable things happened, some good, some not so much so. The first night we lived there, the neighbors' dogs killed my precious cat, Jenny. When school was out, Daddy closed his shop and we went to Indiana and worked for four months in the tomato fields. Inella and I were not allowed to hoe but when it came time to pick the tomatoes, we went to work with the rest of the family. My parents told me that if I would pick 50 hampers of tomatoes a day during picking season, they would buy me a Radio Flyer wagon when we got home. I did and they did. I don't know exactly how much a hamper held, but I tend to think it must have been about a half bushel. I guess 50 hampers or 25 bushels a day for a 7-year-old wasn't bad. And $5 a day wasn't bad either, 70 years ago. We were paid a dime for each hamper we picked. With six of us working, we did quite well that summer, earning enough to pay off the place we had bought at Kirby.

For my seventh birthday in March, my mother's cousin gave me a cute puppy, a genuine full-blood Heinz 57, brown and white with a white-tipped tail that curled over his back. He never seemed to walk when he went anywhere, but rather skipped along like a little school girl. I named him Skippy and we usually called him Skip. He was still a baby when we left for Indiana. He rode in the back of our tarp-covered pickup, along with us four kids and sometimes, Grandpa Turner. Skip was such a joy and lifted our spirits as we worked.

While working in the fields, we were frequently stung by sweat bees. I couldn't help but scream when one stung me and wherever that pup was, he'd come running to check on me. He had a bucket lid or some such that stayed near our water jug in the fields, to drink his water from. One day his lid somehow became lost, so he went out somewhere, possibly to a place where someone had dumped trash near the edge of the field, and found a broken dish. It was damaged, but would still hold enough water to give a pup a drink. So he brought that dish and put it with the water jug in anticipation of the next water break.

One day we went to a little store in a nearby town to buy some groceries. The store's owner had an adorable little girl who came near the truck to see Skip. She was eating an ice cream cone and wanted to give it to him. She said, "It's so hot, I'm afraid he'll wilt." So she gave him the cone and he thanked her nicely. We heard later that she had been bitten by a rabid dog and had to have those horrible shots. It just seemed like such an unfair thing to happen to such a sweet child.

Our nearest neighbor's big red rooster, who was allowed to run loose, had chased Skip every day from the time he came to us till we left for Indiana, making his life miserable. The first thing he did when we finally arrived home was bail out of the truck and head for that rooster. Skip had grown by leaps and bounds in the last four months. It didn't take long for him to establish his place at the top of the local pecking order. The cock of the walk was no longer in charge.

We were late enrolling in school that year at Kirby, but it didn't seem to cause a problem. Surprisingly, I was elected carnival queen for our second-grade class, and my brother was king for his class. He was either a Junior or Senior that year.

Ernie Dunlap's store, the only one in "town" was straight in front of our house, a distance of maybe half a block, on a busy highway. There was a highway intersection just past the store, and the other highway ran beside our house. We walked through the back yard of our nearest neighbor to reach the store (with their blessing) without having to get in the road. I was often sent to the store to get some item, which was put on our account. There was an old man who lived in the country, actually in the same old house my mother had grown up in, and he rode a white mule to the store when he needed something. My dad used to tease my mother about him over a remark the man had made years before. John Hale had married, apparently not well, because his wife had left him with two little girls to raise by himself. He had supposedly made the statement, "I sure messed up. I could have had any one of them nice Turner girls, and look what I done to myself." My mother was "one of them nice Turner girls" and my dad loved teasing her about it.

One day my folks sent me to the store for something and I told them I was tired of the people at the store asking to whom they should charge it, because they knew who I was. So Daddy said if they asked to just tell them to charge it to John Hale. At the time I had never seen John Hale to know him and wasn't aware of the joke. So when they asked me, I told them to charge it to John Hale. The clerk pointed out a silver-haired gentleman across the store and asked me if I knew who the man was. He said it was John Hale, and the store employees had a good laugh about it. How embarrassing!

* * *

That fall I remember coming home from school many days to find my mother shut up in her bedroom, and she appeared to be hustling around inside the room before she came out. I never really thought that much about it, but at Christmas I learned what had been going on. She had bought me a doll for Christmas and made clothing for the doll from scraps of fabric she had used to make dresses for me. I still remember that as one of my best Christmases.

My mother was an excellent seamstress and we three girls were often ahead of our peers where fashion was concerned. But I doubt that anyone ever noticed that. The latest styles never reached our small town quite as soon as they did in larger cities. When a new Sears catalog came out with all the new fashions in it, she'd have us study the new dresses shown in it and pick out the ones we liked best. By looking at a picture, she could make a pattern and turn out dresses that looked identical to the ones shown in the catalog. But we were never completely in style because economy dictated that we wear our shoes completely out before we got new ones, so we were usually ahead on dresses and behind on shoes. Of course, since I was the youngest and wore a lot of hand-me-downs, I was seldom in style with anything. And I never cared.

Back to Heavener

My dad couldn't really make a living in his shop at Kirby because, as my brother told me later, "Too many of his customers were relatives." So he sold out and we moved back to Heavener for the last time. He went to work in the Oldsmobile dealership which was owned by Herman Johnston. Daddy *was* the service department. Later, Veachel, worked there with him. One of them told me a few years ago that Herman never took a dime that was paid in for work they had done. What they earned was all theirs to keep, although Herman provided the tools and the place to work. I have to think it was an advantage for Herman to have good mechanics working for him, but that still would have left him with only the income from cars he sold. Herman remained a good friend of Daddy's as long as they both lived.

At some point, Daddy left the dealership. I don't remember why. Maybe that was when Herman closed it down. But another friend of his, Rufus Montgomery, built him a shop, including a forge, about three doors south of the Oldsmobile place. Daddy paid rent for this shop and was there for a number of years, till crippling rheumatoid arthritis put him down for good. That old shop is still standing, and I noticed yesterday that "Linville Garage" above the north drive door is still readable.

Later, when a medication was found to help him move around a little better, he started working on lawn mowers at home. He said he knew that the steroids might do bad things to him, and would probably shorten his life, but if they would help him get out of bed and do some work, it would be worth it. He thoroughly enjoyed having people from all over the area bring him their mowers to work on. He loved people and I feel his contact with them kept him going for several years.

Losing my Parents

One day a few years later, I went by to see my folks and Daddy was sitting in an old chair out in his garden. He had been putting out tomato plants and had become so exhausted he had to stop. He asked me if I would finish up that job for him, which of course I was happy to do. But it concerned me. The next time he went to his doctor, they ran tests and told him that he had only about 25% of his heart function left. They also told him to quit doing anything that exerted him in the least. But he continued exactly as he had been. One day I went by their house and he was hunched over a lawn mower out by his shop door, working as usual. By then his vision was so bad that he had to work mostly by feel. But he could still fix those mowers and people kept bringing them. I told him, "Daddy, one of these days we're going to find you out here stretched out over one of those mowers—dead."

He said, "I hope you do. That's exactly the way I'd like to go." But it didn't work that way. He became so weak that we could no longer take care of him at home and he eventually wound up in a nursing home. I went every day on my lunch hour from work, fed him his lunch, and gave him a BC powder (aspirin and caffeine) dissolved in his Dr. Pepper, which I kept in his room. He was not allowed to have aspirin, but said it was the only thing that ever gave him any relief. So I made sure he had food in his stomach before I gave him any and if it ever hurt him, I never knew of it. I'm pretty sure some of the nurses knew about it, but they never mentioned it.

He also kept in his room an Absorbine Jr. bottle that had horse liniment in it and used it faithfully. One day the head nurse, a dear, understanding, and compassionate lady, told me that I should take away his "Absorbine Jr." bottle and not bring it back for a couple of days because there was an inspector coming who would probably confiscate it. It hadn't fooled her for a minute, but she had the wisdom to know that people his age usually knew what worked for them and that they should be left alone in such cases.

Every day for three years, I went to the nursing home on my lunch hour from work at the First Baptist Church two blocks south of the nursing home. We lost Mother eight months after she had entered the nursing home. He outlived her by over two years. Every day, I wheeled him to the shower and cleaned him up, cut his hair and nails when needed, changed his bed, took care of every need I could. I often wished he could have gone suddenly while working on mowers rather than having to spend three years huddled in that bed in pain, probably praying to die. But we learn to take what we're given and make the most of it.

Mother had Alzheimer's for many years before she died. Daddy always loved her so much, but in her later years she had him confused with her own father who had abused her horribly when she was growing up. I never saw her as a vengeful person at all, as she was always good to her dad who had outlived her mother by many years. He had lost his farm during the depression, and after Grandma died in 1938, he lived with some of his kids, moving from one to the other till the last few years, when he stayed only with Mother's oldest sister, as she was widowed and needed his company as well.

Mother was never anything but nice to her dad that I saw, but as her dementia progressed over the years, she had him and my dad mixed up in her mind. I know that for sure because she started calling Daddy "Dad" as she had always called Grandpa. And in that state of mind, she made Daddy pay for what her own father had done to her when she was growing up. I won't even go into all that she had to endure, because I was told he changed when his wife died and I never really saw anything much out of him. But now Mother was remembering him as he was when she was a girl. When Mother and Daddy both were in the nursing home at the same time during her last months, Daddy couldn't even see her without her going ballistic.

He sadly told me one day that he had been wanting to see her and asked the nurses to wheel him down to her room, only to hear, "Get him out of here!" I know it hurt Daddy so much, but he just kept on loving her.

One night about 10:00 p.m. our phone rang and it was one of the nurses at the Vista. She said simply, "Honey, I think your mother is gone." I know it was a strange reaction, but all I could think was, "Thank you, Lord." They had put her to bed around 8:00 p.m, and when they did a bed check at 10:00, she was gone. I knew she was out of her misery and was with the Lord.

Soon after she died, a relative started telling him about how mean Mother had been to him. He told me about it and asked, "Was Mother mean to me? I don't remember her ever being mean to me." I thought it was amazing that he instantly forgot all he had been through in the last 20 or more years and had been able to completely put it aside and forgive and forget. I told him that

Mother had loved him so much, but her mind had gone bad and she wasn't responsible for anything hurtful she said to him after that. And he seemed to be able to accept that.

They were married for 65 years and I heard him tell someone after she died that, "We were married for 65 years and were never apart." Never mind what happened when they were together. Now as I look back and think of all the things the two of them had to endure, with problems with some of their children and other people, I think it's a wonder my mother held up as long as she did. Daddy always had a job, even after he was forced to retire and work at home, while Mother had nothing outside the house to take her mind off things.

Memories of World War II

The enemy attack on Pearl Harbor, which drew the U.S. into World War II, happened when I was eight months old, so I never knew how things had been before the war. I vaguely remember hearing talk about things that were rationed, including sugar, tires, and metal of various kinds. I've never understood what caused the shortage of sugar, because I do know sugar beets and sugar cane were grown in mainland U.S., so they should have been a good source of sugar. I'm sure there were logical reasons for it, but at this point it makes no difference. Back then, it made a big difference to people who had a sweet tooth. My mother bought a lot of canned pineapple and pretty much burned us out on pineapple pie. Pineapple supplies enough sugar to make a pie with little or no added sugar, so it was mostly pineapple pie or no sweets.

I remember once when I was three or four and Mother had made a pineapple pie and set the can aside temporarily before she put it in the trash. I picked the can up and was picking bits of pineapple off the inside of the can and most likely was licking the lid as well. No big deal, as I saw it. Suddenly she saw me with that can and freaked out. It seems that at that time the cans were made of some kind of metal that was poison, or at least not good to put in your mouth. Mother made me drink straight vinegar as an antidote. I've never wished for a pineapple pie since then, nor known anyone in my family who cares for it.

Since TV was not yet a commodity enjoyed by most people, and I was too young to read comic books, I have no idea how I knew about bubble gum and balloons, but by the time the war was over, I had heard of them but had never seen either of them. It must have been in 1945 after the end of the war, that Veachel heard that some little store "across town" had bubble gum and balloons and he rode his bicycle to buy some for us kids. I can't recall being all that impressed with them.

During WWII, I often heard my mother talking about the war and her two nephews who were overseas. Delbert Babbitt was a prisoner in a German prisoner of war camp for quite a long time. His parents were sent word that he was missing in action, and they were, of course, devastated. After some time, a woman my aunt knew, who lived in another part of the state, came to see my aunt and brought her a newspaper. On the front of the paper was a picture said to have been made from a small plane flying low over a large enclosure, supposedly a prisoner of war camp in Germany. The pilot no doubt had taken his life in his hands to attempt such a thing, but he did get very clear pictures of prisoners in the courtyard. The visitor asked my aunt if a particular man in the picture was her son. She was sure it was and said so. That brought an amazing amount of peace to her and her family. When Delbert finally got home and was asked if he might remember having seen an American plane flying low over his prison, he said he did and that he was out in the courtyard at the time.

Delbert had been an average sized man when he left home, but by the time he was freed from that prison, he weighed 86 pounds.

His brother was in the unit that freed him and his fellow prisoners. I remember hearing that Delbert saw his brother and recognized him, but his brother didn't know him. I wonder if perhaps Delbert had long hair and a beard by then. From things I heard about the treatment he had received, I can't imagine his captors being overly generous with such things as combs and razor blades. But maybe the weight loss alone changed his looks enough to make him unrecognizable.

When the liberators came into the area where Delbert was at the time, he saw his brother, picked up a broom and started sweeping the floor, trying to be in his brother's way every way he turned. His brother kept trying to step around him and do what he was supposed to be doing. Finally, Delbert looked his brother squarely in the face and said, "Don't you know me?" I've often imagined the emotions those two experienced at that point. I was told that the prisoners, once freed by their compatriots, rushed into the kitchen and ate everything they could get their hands on. Delbert reportedly ate a whole pound of butter. I can't imagine ever being hungry enough to do that, but then I've never been that hungry, either. I'm just so thankful that he was freed from that prison when he was. He didn't live to be old, but did have a few good years with his wife and children after returning home.

The Worst School Teacher Ever

We moved back to Heavener in the middle of the year when I was in the second grade. I was always an independent little toot and I didn't need a parent to go with me to enroll in school. At least I didn't have one and that was fine with me. My older brother drove me to school across town from the high school where he attended and let me out. I knew the second grade teachers from the year before and knew the one I wanted. I went inside, entered Mrs. Wynn's room, put my lunch in the cabinet used for that purpose, found a seat, and made myself at home. When the rest of the kids came in, confusion reigned. The teacher was especially confused. How did I get there? Who had brought me? And what was she to do with me? So the office was consulted and it was determined it was NOT Mrs. Wynn's turn to have a new student. I shudder still to think about where I wound up.

For obvious reasons, I dare not mention the name of the teacher whose class I was sent to. In all my years of school, I had many good teachers, a few not so good, and this one, whom I'll refer to as Mrs. X. That lady was scary! She would throw a temper fit, grow red in the face, stomp her feet, hit anyone unfortunate enough to be within her reach, and throw things at students. I can still remember her hurling blackboard erasers across the room at some boys who were getting on her nerves. I was terrified of her, and I feel sure others felt the same way.

I remember once when we were having a test, she warned us that no one was to speak a word or leave their seat, or they would pay the consequences. She got busy on papers on her desk and never raised her head for anything. Of course right away my pencil lead broke and I could write no more. I waved my hand around in the air for what seemed like an eternity and still she never looked up. So I was sitting there weighing the options: flunk the test and give her the broken-pencil-lead excuse, or risk tiptoeing up to her desk and whispering for permission to sharpen my pencil. I chose the latter and lived to regret it. She whirled on me with eyes flashing and yelled, "YOU MAY SIT DOWN!" as she whopped me so hard it almost knocked me down. I literally felt my eyes cross as I retreated to my seat. I have no idea what happened after that, as I must have been absolutely comatose. I later saw the scene repeated with another girl, and yes, her eyes did cross. I never told my folks about it, but I later wished I had.

At the time, my mother was trying to follow the teaching of some new preacher with whom we had come into contact, and he preached that it was a sin for girls and women to wear pants. So my sisters and I did not wear pants during that time. I also had chronic bronchitis for 10 years and my mother forbade me to go outside when it was cold. So I had to stay inside at every recess. Mrs. X resented that in no small way. We were also not allowed to attend movies at the time—again thanks to that particular preacher.

The local theater at one point was good enough to put on a free show for all the school kids. All of them except me, of course. I was forbidden to go. I wonder why my folks didn't just keep me home that day. I think it would have better for all concerned. But that wasn't the way it worked. Looking back now, I'm thinking I probably didn't even mention it at home, knowing what the answer would be. When I told my teacher I couldn't go, she unleashed all the built-up fury she had for me in one thorough tongue lashing.

She said, "You can't go to movies. You can't wear pants. You come over here every day in those little old thin dresses and you have to stay in, which means I have to stay in with you." She went on and on for what seemed like hours. Bear in mind that she's talking to a seven-year-old child. I don't remember much about the rest of that day or what happened, but I do know I did not attend that movie.

After that, I was afraid to stay in at recess, and afraid to go out for fear my mother would find out. So I entered the cloak room with the rest of the kids when they went in to get their coats, and then I stayed there till they came back in. I would stand quietly in the cloak room, almost afraid to breathe, fearing she would find me in there and attack. A few times she did come to the cloak room to get something, and I would oh-so-quietly slip out one door as she entered the other, then repeat the process when she went out. I was never caught, but lived in constant fear that I would be.

I need to mention here the reason for my choosing not to tell my parents about this teacher. It went back to an incident that had happened when my oldest sister was in the first grade. One first grade class was located in the building with the upper grades, which was on the opposite side of town from the grade school. I'm sure that was done to keep little ones on that side of town from needing to walk across the railroad and the busy highway. We lived on the side of town where the high school was located so when she started to school, they naturally enrolled her in that class.

One very cold day, my mother had sent her to school in overalls. I don't know if they belonged to my brother or where they came from, because we girls never wore pants back in those days. But Mother thought she needed the warmth. The story was that the teacher yelled at her for wearing them and "shook her." Teachers used to shake kids when they were angry. Now it would be a federal offense. My sister went home at noon and told our parents about it, and Daddy went straight to the school in search of that teacher. It may be best that she wasn't there. Daddy didn't often get mad, but as they used to say, when he did, he was mad all over.

In any case, he told the principal why he was there and what would happen if his child were ever again punished for something that wasn't even her fault. We never knew what happened at the school after he left. Neither Inella nor I were put in that teacher's class when we started to school, but when we got in higher grades, that same teacher did everything in her power to get us in trouble. She was put in charge of the cafeteria at noon so she picked on both of us in there. She tried to cause Inella trouble as she worked in the cafeteria. She picked on me while I tried to eat there (students from Westside School were bussed across town to eat at the high school cafeteria) accusing me of misbehavior and separating me from the others, although I was doing nothing different from what they were doing. She just looked for anything to embarrass us or cause us trouble. So from then on, we thought it best to suffer in silence when we had problems with a teacher and not risk causing trouble for any of the family later on.

I hung on day by day, living for the end of school. I had my mind made up that the next year I would be in Miss Himes' class and I lived for that day. She was a dear, sweet, kind woman and I so looked forward to being in her class.

But it was not to be. Think "Groundhog Day." The first day in Miss Himes' class, the principal came to our class and said my teacher from the year before did not have enough second-grade students for a full class, so she would be teaching a split class of second and third graders. And she was allowed to choose the third graders from students she had had the year before. I never knew for sure how those choices were made, but I believed she chose the ones she knew she already had thoroughly intimidated. And of course I fell into that group.

By the grace of God I survived that year, but I can't stand to think about it now. It was just too awful.

Mrs. Stuart, Wonderful Teacher

When I was in the fourth grade, my home room teacher was Mrs. Stuart. I had known her husband from the Marvin Stuart Dry Goods store and her sweet daughter, Kaye, who was ahead of me in school. But I had never met Mrs. Stuart since she was either teaching elsewhere or had taken a break from teaching. She was such a nice lady and I loved her dearly. I had a thing at the time about making all A's and she had at one point not given anyone an A in penmanship. I think she must have been pretty disgusted with the whole class at the time for being sloppy writers. I'm not saying I deserved an A, but I was disappointed. Later in the year, somehow I lost my report card before I returned it to her after taking it home at the end of the six weeks period. It was the only time I ever lost one. I had no choice but to tell her about losing it and she was forced to fill out a new one for me. Had she been the teacher I had in the second and third grades, she would probably have killed me. But instead, she said, "You know, I've always thought I should have given you an A in penmanship the first time and I'm going to fix that now." So she gave me A's all that year, from the first grading period through the last. It didn't make a lot of difference in the grand scheme of things, but somehow it just gave me a warm feeling. I wished I could have had a teacher like her every year.

A Love Story

When I was in school everybody knew that Miss Owens liked Mr. Keller. Liked him a lot. In fact, I'm sure she really loved him. Everybody knew it for a couple of generations. But not everybody was still in Heavener decades later to see her prove it.

I'll have to admit that in school I had trouble warming up to Miss Owens. I'm sure she meant well, and she never did anything to me, but I just found it hard to get close to her.

Mr. Keller, on the other hand, was a dear, dear man as far as I was concerned. I found his willingness to share his faith appealing, and till the end of his life I considered him to be a good friend.

Even after they had both retired from teaching, Mr. Keller and Miss Owens were still together almost every time I saw either of them. He drove her to Poteau to Wal-Mart and I would guess for doctors' appointments or anywhere she might need to go. As far as I knew, she never owned a car, and may have never had a drivers' license. I sometimes met her walking up the hill to her home on the west side of town. Come to think of it, I even stopped one time to give her a ride. I was surprised that she never changed in appearance. To me she looked the same the last time I saw her as she did the first time. Mr. Keller lived in the old home place with his brother, Bob, for the rest of his life.

I don't know whether it's fact or fiction, but I was told when I was still a child that Mr. Keller had once been engaged to a girl, probably in college. But she refused to move to Heavener with him and he refused to live anywhere else. There must have been more than that to the story, but he supposedly said after that that he would never marry. And he never did. I tend to believe that story.

When I was working as secretary at the First Baptist Church in the 90's, Mr. Keller, who lived across the street from the church, came into my office one day and told me he had just been told that he had a "mass" in his abdominal area. He was obviously very upset. My heart broke for him, but of course there was nothing I could do for him but pray.

As his health deteriorated and he spent time in the hospital, I often went to see him. Miss Owens was always by his side, fussing over him and doing everything she could to make him comfortable. I was surprised one day when she opened up to me and told me things about his condition that I was surprised to hear her discuss. She had found it necessary to step in and help where most men would have a wife or daughter to look after them. But she was all he had, and she never let him down.

One day I went to see Mr. Keller at Poteau hospital and Miss Owens was not there. His door was standing open, and he was lying there in bed on his back, apparently staring at the ceiling. For the first time, he didn't turn his head to speak and reach out a hand. It took only a few seconds for me to realize he was gone. I couldn't believe he had been left lying there, with the door open for people to walk in and receive the shock I had received. I don't know what the situation was. Maybe I called a nurse and she said they already knew it. Maybe not. I was in such a state of shock that I pretty much blocked out everything.

I wondered what would become of Miss Owens with Mr. Keller no longer around. I didn't have to wonder long. She loaded up and moved to Durant, where her brother lived. There was no doubt in my mind that she had stayed in Heavener for her beloved "B.J.", even knowing he would never marry her.

How very sad for her. How sad for both of them. But to me she proved what real love is—loving a man forever even with the knowledge that it could never be more to him than friendship.

I wish I had gone to the trouble to get to know her better. I feel she must have been one of the most misunderstood and underappreciated people I've ever known. Not knowing her better was my loss. I hope I've learned from it.

Neighbors on East Ave. B

We had such good neighbors on East Ave. B. Across the street from us to the south were the Hudlows. There was Lonzo, who was also our postman, who could do anything, his wife Iona Mae, who could play the piano like a dream, their oldest child, Chuck, oldest daughter, Patricia, and the baby, Judy. A few years later they had Joyce Ann, who was such a delight. She learned to walk young and no one could keep her down. One day Lonzo was working on the roof, perhaps putting up a TV antenna, when he looked up and saw her toddling down the peak of the roof towards him. I'm thinking she was nine months old at the time, but she might have been a little older. She was very young, in any case. Lonzo just froze, afraid to approach her for fear of causing her to fall, so he just told her, "Come here and hand me that wrench, Joyce," which she did. I was fortunate enough to get to babysit them all at times, and I loved it.

Not long after Joyce was born, perhaps a couple of months, the neighbors across from us to the west, Hugh and Ruth Gardenhire, had a new son. And a few days later, my mother gave me the little brother I had dreamed of having for years. No one was ever happier to have a younger sibling. It still seems strange that families on three of four adjacent corners had babies within two months' time.

Phil Gardenhire became a famous rodeo announcer and the arena in Poteau, our county seat, is named for him. Phil had the most amazing bass voice and also preached at places around the area. He was a good man and well thought of. Tragically, Phil was killed a number of years ago when a vehicle going at a high rate of speed roared across the railroad tracks and the highway without stopping, and hit Phil's truck. As I recall, he was killed instantly. Phil had one son, Tyler, who grew up and married my great niece, Lee Ann, Inella's granddaughter. He is a wonderful husband and dad, and Lee Ann is a wonderful wife, mother, and school teacher. They have three of the cutest kids ever and they are such a special family.

It seems strange to think how Phil, Joyce, and Rick were all born within about a month, and all three of them died comparatively young. Joyce was the last of the three to leave this old vale of tears, and I believe she was in her early 60's at the time.

The Gardenhires also had Larry and Glenda Gail. Larry was one of my horse-back riding buddies later on. The Upchurch's lived across the street in front of the Gardenhire's. Next door to the Upchurch's lived Paul and Ione Johnston and their daughter, Paulann, who was in my class in school. Later they had Johnny. Anyone who knows Johnny could write a book about him. He's one of the funniest people you could ever hope to meet. Next door to the west lived the Pete Bains. They were the parents of Ione Johnston.

West of the Gardenhires lived the Warner's, Bill and Emmagene, and their two sons, Billy Paul and Dick. West of them was the Ralph Anderson family Ralph, Reba Doris, and kids Karen and Carl. The Upchurch's were Reba Doris' parents. Karen grew up to become the director of the local Mental Health clinic. West of them, after a couple of years, Irene Fielder and her kids moved into the big two-story house. I'm not sure if she had married Aaron Roop by that time or not. I thought it was strange that so many of our neighbors on East First Street later became our neighbors on East Ave. B.

At the end of the block lived Mr. and Mrs. Bill Robinson. She was one of the local piano teachers and I had maybe a dozen lessons from her. They had one son, Gillan Dean, who just had his 90th birthday yesterday. Everyone calls him Gilly as they have for decades. He is a good man and a good friend of ours. His wife, Bettye, passed away a number of years ago and today his lady friend is also Betty, who is our next-door neighbor, and whose husband, Norris Burns, passed away about the same time as Gilly's wife. Gilly lives around the corner from us and he and Betty help each other with mowing their large lawns and keep an eye out for each other health-wise. Betty Burns still plays senior basketball on a team that plays in other states, and she also still walks and runs in races. I suppose she always wins in her age category. She's a living testimony to what walking every day of our life can accomplish health-wise.

Some other neighbors on East Ave. B were the Alva Roop family and Bud Faulkenberry and his precious wife, Alice. Next door we again had the Black's for neighbors. Lewie Brown and his family lived behind us. Ray Brown was their cute little boy and Ruth Ellen was the teen-aged daughter. Our phone number at the time was 431 Red. The Brown's number was 431 Black. My mother used to tell people, when giving them our phone number, "Be sure and say "Red" or the operator might give you "Black" and you'll get Brown's."

Ray Brown and I grew up as playmates and after we were older, we remained friends, although I was several years older than he was. One night when I was in high school we had played basketball out of town and were late getting back. At such times I would walk home alone from town where the school bus let us out at the Coffee Shop, staying right in the middle of the street, swiveling my neck from side to side to avoid any surprises from—anything frightening. I had to walk several blocks and normally didn't meet another person. That night I suddenly heard a blood curdling scream and saw something rise up out of the road ditch. It turned out to be Ray and he thought he had really pulled a good one on me. I still owe him for that!

Alva and Loneta Roop had two boys, Bill, the little red-headed, curly-haired one, and John, who looked more like his dad. When I was about eight or nine years old, Bill frequently came over to our house and asked, "Will you take me to the store?" I can still see his little sandaled feet coming up our old wooden steps as he talked. I would walk with him down to Melvin Walker's store about three blocks west of us. John was younger and I didn't get to know him that well before they built a house out in the country and moved. But they didn't stay there long before they built another house down on East First Street and moved back into town.

Tom and Dora Trent, Like Grandparents

After the Roops moved away, her aunt who lived up the street and on top of the hill, Mrs. Trent, moved in their house across from us. Mr. Trent had passed away some time before. Mrs. Trent was the nearest thing to a grandmother that I ever had. I loved her dearly. But for a few years prior to that, I was just plain jealous of her. Mr. Trent kept cows and had a milk route, which he delivered in a rubber-tired wagon. In the summertime and on days when there was no school, I was his helper on the milk wagon. I thought it was the greatest thing ever, and never realized till I was older and having more trouble getting around, how much help I must have been to him. He was always giving me gifts, like when I got a good report card. I still have a little dress, to me the best one Mother ever made for me, that she made from feed sacks he had given me.

He also kept chickens and geese and ducks and would sometimes give us a goose egg. Before we knew he had the geese and ducks, he once told us that he only had 12 chickens but had gotten 14 eggs that day. When he suddenly died, I was devastated. I had never even bothered to get to know his sweet wife till after he was gone, but later came to love her as much as I had him. Their son was Kester Trent, who coached football for Heavener for years. Kester's wife played the piano for First Baptist Church, and their daughter was Tommie Kay, named for her grandfather. The elder Trents also had daughters, Ada Ruth and Billie June, who lived in another state and I never really got to know them well.

One thing I remember about Mrs. Trent was the time when Mother had made me a new dress, supposedly in the new "princess style." I don't know if Mother had ever actually seen anyone in a princess style dress. I'm guessing she made it from pictures in a catalog. At the time, I was young and had at least the suggestion of a figure, unlike what I'm living with now. The dress fit me more like a sack dress and I was almost embarrassed to wear it. One day I went over to Mrs. Trent's house for something and she commented on the dress—nicely, of course. I told her that it was supposed to be more fitted, but Mother didn't want to take it up to fit that way. I was surprised to hear Mrs. Trent say, "Well, you tell her if she doesn't want to do it, I'll do it." Mrs. Trent was always so kind to everyone, and she was kind in that case. But she would have done it. I don't remember what Mother said when I mentioned it again, but she took it up so it fit.

Mrs. Trent was from Tennessee and had some different ways of saying things. She wouldn't say, "Do you like" (some food) but would say, "Do you love" that food. I loved her so much. She filled every requirement I would ever have had for a grandmother if I could have chosen.

Tragedy in the Neighborhood

One day we saw a sudden flurry of police cars at the house on the far side of the Brown's behind us. On investigation, we learned that the man in that house was down in his yard, having been shot by the neighbor across the street from them. The story was that the man across the street, who shall remain nameless for the sake of his family, was angry at Mr. Bain because he thought Mr. Bain had told someone else about his secret hunting spot that he had shared with Mr. Bain. So he just shot him from across the street. Mr. Bain was down and his wife came to the door, planning to go out and see about him. But he yelled at her to stay inside, saying he could get up but wouldn't do so for fear of being shot again. At this point, the neighbor turned the gun on himself. What a horrible experience for several people! I feel sure the old man who did the shooting must have had a mental breakdown because I had never heard of any sign of violence in him before that. He had a sweet wife and it must have been an unimaginable shock for her.

Many years later, a friend of my niece was living in a house that was built on the same lot that the shooter's house had been on before it was torn down. Her family knew nothing about the history of the house originally on that site. But they started seeing and hearing strange things in that house, things they couldn't explain, and it made them very uneasy. So they moved out. People who knew about it wondered if the house could be haunted. I don't know about things like that, but it would make you wonder. I've often looked at that house when we drove by it, and it never seems to be occupied. I'd love to know what's going on there.

Charlotte, the Horses and Me

My friend, Charlotte Johnston, who is a cousin to Paulann, lived on East Ave. A, which was one block north of East Ave. B, but by going out our back door, cutting across East 6th street, down the alley, and through her back yard, her house was just a hop and a skip from mine. Charlotte's dad was the local cobbler (shoe repairman) and ran a shop downtown. Her mother was a beautiful Cherokee lady and the sweetest one ever. When we were in our Sophomore year of high school, we both had horses and sometimes rode together. Her next-door neighbors were the Frizzell brothers, Johnny and Glennie, and sometimes we all went riding together, along with Larry Gardenhire, Phil's older brother. Larry had Phil on a horse with him from the time Phil could barely sit up, and Phil became quite a horseman when he grew up. For what it's worth, they were all considerably younger than we were. The Frizzell's had a younger brother, Michael, but he was too young to join us at the time. Sadly, Johnny and Glennie both passed away in recent years.

Charlotte later moved to Edmond, OK. I've been blessed to visit her there a few times since she moved back from California.

Cleaning the Wood Floors

I was about eleven or twelve when my parents went somewhere for the day and left me and my two older sisters home alone. I decided I would give the house a real cleaning and have a surprise waiting for them when they got home.

One of the first things I decided to do was to clean the wood floor in the living room and dining room. This was real wood, not the laminated kind they sell so much of now with the top layer of formica-type material.

I looked under the sink to see what kinds of cleaners Mother had on hand. I could sum them up in two words—not many. I did find a container of Spic and Span, which to those who aren't familiar with the product, can be a type of scouring powder, if you choose to use it the way I did instead of dissolving it in water. I'm not sure if they even make it in that form these days.

I moved all the furniture, wet mopped the floor, sprinkled on Spic and Span, and started scrubbing. A couple of hours later, the floor was rinsed and I thought looked pretty good. I could hardly wait for my parents to see it. They would be so happy.

Recently we've been discussing the pros and cons of wood

floors. My husband has always been afraid of them, saying any spill or water leak could ruin them, but I really like them. However, after recently reading about the special care they require, I finally understand why my parents decided to have the floors refinished shortly after my cleaning spree.

Heavener's Doctors

Through the years, Heavener has had a number of good doctors. I remember Dr. Fair, Dr. Harvey, Dr. Hogaboom, Dr. Looper, and a few others, the last one being Dr. Schumpert, who moved away a couple of years ago. Many of us old-timers think Dr. Hogaboom was one of the best doctors Heavener has ever had.

Unfortunately, too many people remember him as much for his problem as for his doctoring skills. Dr. Hogaboom had a drinking problem. I was told that he had been an army doctor during World War II, and he would stand in one spot and operate on wounded servicemen so long that when he finally finished, he couldn't move his feet. He had to be helped to a chair or maybe to bed. He supposedly started drinking to be able to keep going past the limits of normal human endurance. Every time I watch an episode of "MASH" on TV, where the doctors who served during the Korean War worked for long hours trying to save the lives of wounded soldiers, I think of Dr. Hogaboom. When the war was over and he went into private practice, it was hard for him to give up the alcohol.

My family had lots of experience with Dr. Hogaboom. He was the one who delivered my little brother in 1952. At the time,

Heavener had a small hospital, and it was there my mother went to give birth. Dr. Hogaboom was resting in a room across the hall when his nurse decided it was time for him to make his appearance and take care of the actual delivery. When he started across the hall to Mother's room, the nurse had to escort him back to the room where he had been resting. He had forgotten to put on his pants. But in spite of his inebriated condition, Mother, at the age of 42, had the easiest delivery she had ever had, and this was the sixth live baby she had given birth to.

When my little brother was five months old, he became very sick one night and was having difficulty breathing. He was small and frail and my parents didn't think he would live till morning. They had lost their second daughter to pneumonia and several of us kids had had it later. My dad tried repeatedly to call Dr. Hogaboom, but couldn't get him on the phone. Finally, in desperation, he called our neighbor, Lonzo Hudlow, who delivered mail to Dr. Hogaboom's house, and so knew where he lived. They felt that he was home but not hearing the phone. His wife often visited out-of-town relatives, so they felt that he would be alone.

Daddy and Lonzo drove over to Dr. Hogaboom's house, went inside (people didn't always lock their doors back then) into his bedroom, and woke him up. He immediately started saying, "I didn't hear that phone." He knew they would have called before coming to his house.

They put him in the shower to sober him up, helped him dress, and drove him to our house. He examined my little brother and promptly diagnosed his condition as pneumonia. My parents were devastated and started crying, but Dr. Hogaboom said, "Oh, we don't lose babies to pneumonia anymore." He gave the baby a huge shot of penicillin in his bony little thigh, and by morning he was starting to improve.

When I was a senior in high school, I injured my knee in a basketball game one night. By morning it was full of fluid. My friend, Charlotte, drove me to Dr. Hogaboom's office. She planned to be a nurse and wanted to watch him work on me. He put a shot in my knee to deaden it, then pulled out a huge needle and proceeded to drain the knee, which wasn't easy, considering that I had fallen asleep under a heat lamp the night before and congealed the fluid. My friend fainted. I felt no pain.

Later that afternoon Dr. Hogaboom called our house and asked my mother how I was feeling. He said I should be feeling a lot of pain, and I suppose he was going to prescribe some pain medicine. But I was fine.

A few years after Dr. Hogaboom moved away, I injured the other knee and went to our new doctor. He drained the knee, but it was a different story from before. Suffice it to say I felt enough pain for that procedure plus the one Dr. Hogaboom had done.

Most people who knew Dr. Hogaboom said they would rather have him drunk than any other doctor sober. Even when he was completely stoned, he could give a shot that you would never feel. I'm not sure how it would have been had he been sober.

There was an incident where Dr. Hogaboom delivered a premature baby at the Heavener hospital, and had it in his car rushing it to the hospital at Poteau where an incubator was available. A couple of miles north of town, he hit a horse. Somebody came along and offered to help, and his only concern was getting the baby, which had not been injured, to the hospital. He took the baby and got in the car with the Good Samaritan and asked to be driven to the Poteau Hospital. As far as I know, the baby survived and thrived.

I'm sure there were some people who didn't carc for Dr. Hogaboom. But there are many who did. A few years ago a man told me that back in the 50's his brother had been very ill. I've always thought he must have had polio. They would have Dr. Hogaboom out to the house to see him one day, then the next day they might have a different doctor, depending on who was available.

One day Dr. Hogaboom told the boy's parents that they needed to take him to University Hospital in Oklahoma City, and if they didn't, they were going to lose him. The dad told him they had no car and no money. Dr. Hogaboom pulled $80 out of his wallet, ($80 was a sizeable amount back then) gave it to the man, and told him to hire somebody to take the boy to the hospital. He knew it wasn't likely that the people could ever pay him back, but that didn't seem to matter to him. They hired somebody to take the boy to the hospital, where he spent weeks in an iron lung. He eventually recovered, and his family gave Dr. Hogaboom credit for saving his life.

We live in a new world now where few doctors can afford to have a private practice and usually have nothing to do with how their patients are billed. There are still doctors who have a heart, but I don't expect to ever have another one like Dr. Hogaboom.

Incidentally, I was told that years after leaving Heavener, the good doctor was finally able to lick his drinking habit, and where he had been skin and bones when we knew him, he had gained a lot of weight. I'm sure the change was good for him and his family, but most of us were happy with him just the way he was.

My Baby Brother

All my life I had yearned and prayed for a baby brother. My older brother married at 18 and a couple of years later he and his sweet wife had a little boy. They named him Ronnie Merle and I sure did love him. Then, what a surprise to learn that my mother was expecting as well! She gave birth to a fragile little boy who was given the name of Ricky Earl. I wondered if she had wanted to name Veachel after Daddy (Earl) and he didn't want one named after him, but 21 years later decided it might be all right to do so. My brothers were born 21 years and three days apart. Ron was 10 months older than Rick and because of the way their birthdays fell, they went through all 12 of their school years together in the same class. Many people were confused about it, thinking they were brothers or even twins, although they bore no resemblance to each other at all. Some thought Ron was Rick's uncle, instead of the other way around.

My niece, Sherry, was born in 1954 and she was a joy of another kind. The three of them had great times together. I often thought of the Beverly Hillbillies when Ron and Sherry got going. She was a tiny little blonde thing like Ellie Mae Clampett and she could clobber her older brother when he needed it as Ellie Mae used to do to Jethro. Ron was something of a schemer where his sister was concerned, so she learned to just whip up on him when she didn't like something he did.

I used to ride my bicycle all over our side of town with Rick on my right arm, steering with my left. He was cute and witty and musically inclined from birth and just a joy to have around. When he was a tiny baby, on his back in his crib, if he heard music, he kept time to it with his right hand. Years later he could tune a piano without even using a tuning fork because he had perfect pitch. It used to aggravate me that he would come into a room where I was trying to play the piano and announce what key I was playing in. I had to look at the music sheet and figure out what key I was playing in. But he knew it when he heard it and he was always right.

When he was older, he played music at different places around the area and was often called on to play for people to sing. He played the guitar well, but was most often asked to play the piano, as he could find the key and play along with anyone on any song they chose to sing. I once heard him playing for a man who had a wonderful voice but sometimes had a hard time staying on key. The man would wander off key and Rick would pause for a minute, then rejoin him in the key he had changed to. His specialty was "Last Date" and he sounded just like Floyd Cramer. Rick also learned to play the banjo and harmonica a bit.

Veachel and Ron also played the guitar and the three of them had some good musical times together.

Before Rick was born, the four of us older kids often sang together. There were a few times when we were asked to sing on local radio programs. Daddy liked to take Inella and me to "singings" at various churches around the area and put us up there to sing a duet. We continued that for years after we both married. I had a feeling that we weren't that great and would have preferred to stop doing it, but it meant a lot to Inella so I stayed with it.

The last time we sang together there was to be a singing at Double Branch church near Monroe, and Inella had her heart set on it. So we went over there, got up and did our thing, and sat down. Immediately after that, four adult sisters got up and sang. They were so good that I wanted to hide my face in embarrassment. If I had heard them first, there would have been no way I would have tried to sing that day. So that was it for me. Never again.

Rick had a stroke and heart attack at the age of 39 and was in really bad health after that. But he did live to be 63 and had a pretty good life. He never married but it wasn't by choice. Since he was sickly, Mother was extremely overprotective of him, and the rest of us always thought she had done him a disfavor by not making or even letting him grow up. Daddy would try to get her to loosen up on him, "The boy needs to get out and do things and go places," but she was just too worried about him to loosen up. She drifted into dementia when she was still quite young, and a few years before she died, she lost the ability to recognize her family members, even Rick. After that, Rick got out more, usually to places where country music was played, with Daddy's blessing. Mother died 22 years before Rick did and a couple of years before Daddy did. That left Clem and me with the job of trying to help Rick cope with life in the real world. I'll just say it wasn't easy. Some of us decided that he might have been autistic to some degree, which made life really hard for him. Maybe Mother knew something we didn't.

After our parents died, Rick made little effort to take care of himself. Clem and I rented an apartment for him, bought him new furniture which didn't carry the smell of mold as the old house and furniture in it did, and the family moved him into the apartment.

By then the lawn had grown up and the yard was littered with dead tree limbs and other trash. Our son worked three days with a chainsaw just trying to get it to where it could be mowed. Rick could have mowed it, but just didn't care. We cleaned the place up and sold it at the first opportunity. I wouldn't say Rick was happy in an apartment, but it was better for him. He lived in that apartment for 17 years before he had to enter a nursing home. Since Heavener's last remaining nursing home was closed for remodeling, he had no choice but to go to the Oaks at Poteau. People there were mostly kind to him and in general took good care of him. But it seemed that things went south after a few months. The place was no longer kept as clean as before, and some of the workers seemed less than ideal.

I know nursing homes are often a good thing, but I feel sorry for anyone who has to live in one and has no family members to check on them. In Rick's case, Clem and I went to see about him one day and he said he was feeling really bad. That wasn't unusual, but he seemed especially down that day. A male attendant came in and Rick asked him if he would refill his water cup that he carried with him at all times. All he asked for was a little ice since the water had become warm. I had often seen him sip from that cup but never drink a lot of water at a time. That attendant started chewing on him like nothing I had ever heard. He told Rick that his lungs were filled with fluid—that he was waterlogged from drinking so much water, etc. etc. And he didn't say it nicely. He said, "You keep that cup with you constantly and swig enough water to drown yourself." Rick had a doctor's appointment that day and when the doctor saw him, he sent him to the hospital. After they had checked him over, I asked them if he had too much fluid in his body, as the attendant had said. They looked at me like I had just arrived from Mars and said, "No. In fact, he's badly dehydrated."

At the time, both of Heavener's nursing homes had been vacated while they rebuilt and added to the Vista. I had told Rick that as soon as they got the new one opened, he could be moved to the Vista. I had even had his name put on a waiting list. But he never lived to make the move. That day he took a turn for the worse and wound up in the hospital for the last time. When he was in ICU at Sparks hospital in Fort Smith for the last two weeks of his life, he was so weak he couldn't even raise a hand. Since he was on a ventilator, they gave me a card to hold for him to try to point to letters to spell out what he wanted to say. I had to hold up his arm for him to be able to even point at letters. Finally he was able to spell out, "Let me die."

That was a terrible two weeks for us all. They took out the vent three times, and when it was obvious he could not live without it, a nurse told me that if it was put back in, it would be permanent and he would have to have a tube inserted for feeding. We had watched my sister Inella deal with a feeding tube for years before she died at age 54, and so hoped that would not be the case with Rick. So I asked them to please not put the vent back. The nurse looked relieved and said okay and immediately they started unhooking all the tubes, etc. from him. A few minutes later Clem, my niece Renee, and I were in his room, and they told us he was dying. His eyes were fixed on the ceiling, but he showed no sign at all of knowing anything. Suddenly he lifted his right hand and with his arm fully extended, reached for the ceiling, where five minutes earlier he hadn't been able to lift his hand at all. We believed he was seeing Jesus or an angel and were relieved to see him going to meet the Lord. He died minutes later.

High school teachers

Our Freshman home-ec class was quite an experience for those of us who found ourselves faced with a strange teacher on the first day of school. By strange, I mean unfamiliar and well…strange. Miss McCracken was obviously from sturdy old Irish stock. I was never told this, but I figured out for myself that she had attended college at Notre Dame where she was a powerful linebacker for the Fighting Irish. She had the coloration of the Irish, and was anything but a dainty little lady who had majored in Home Ec. I often marveled that she hadn't chosen to coach football or at least teach shop or Vo Ag. I guessed her to be around forty, and she was unmarried at the time. She was not a person to beat around the bush. You always knew exactly where she stood on an issue, even if you didn't care to know. I was told that in one of the other classes on the first day of school, upon hearing one girl's name, she said, "Well, I guess that beats no name at all."

She was known to inquire about the bathing and dressing habits of her students. One day I heard her dispute a girl's answer to her rude questions by pointing out that, "From seeing how nasty your bra straps are, I find that hard to believe." The unit on cooking was a nightmare for most of us. She chose to let us learn some things the hard way. Like how much food to cook for a given number of people. One group cooked too much chicken and made too much whipped cream. She assigned one girl the task of eating all the leftover chicken, and one to eat the remaining whipped cream. The one assigned to eat the chicken surreptitiously slipped it into the trash. Miss McCracken had apparently been around long enough to know what to expect. She retrieved the chicken from the trash and forced the girl to eat it. For some reason I went into the kitchen where I saw one of my friends gagging as she tried to get the rich whipped cream down. She cast pleading eyes on me and said, "Help me." Fortunately for both of us, whipped cream was more easily disposed of than fried chicken. It took only a minute to wash it down the sink drain. Miss McCracken tried to persuade me to give up basketball and take voice lessons from her friend who was our music teacher at the time. Maybe I should have taken her advice on that matter. While I would never have amounted to much as a singer, I might have fewer aches and pains to deal with now, many of which started with a knee injury in basketball.

* * *

One day she asked me if, when I swept a floor, I swept under the bed and other furniture or just swept a trail through the house. I told her I swept under things, to which she predicted, "You'll make a nice finicky old maid."

When it was time to elect officers in FHA, we made our usual campaign speeches in the auditorium. I was running for song leader. I got up on the stage and made some asinine remark and the crowd roared. Every time I opened my mouth the laughter got louder. It was like yelling "sic 'em" to a dog in a room full of cats.

Gee, I had no idea I was so funny. I was on a roll. Eventually I left the stage convinced that I was headed for a life of success as a stand-up comic. When I reached my seat, my friend said, "Do you know why everyone was laughing?"

"Uh…no?" I said.

"As soon as you got up there somebody in the back said, 'She looks just like Miss McCracken,' and everybody heard it." Needless to say I was crushed. While I might share Miss McCracken's Irish background and coloration, at the time she would have made at least two of me. I have no idea what inspired the remark from the back of the room.

But I had had a couple of glorious minutes when I knew how it felt to be a famous entertainer. After having that validation revoked, winning the FHA office seemed a hollow victory.

Mrs. Strickland

After my disappointments with Home Ec class that year, I vowed never to take it again, so when I pre-enrolled, I did not sign up for Home Ec. The next year about the time to enroll for school, there was a new young lady attending our church and I was told she would be our new Home Ec teacher. She seemed so nice that I changed my schedule to include Home Ec. She was such a dear lady and so patient with a student who would have done better in shop than in Home Ec. My sewing project was a corduroy straight skirt. I cut it out and sewed it together, but the pleats just bunched up and stuck out. I picked them out and did them over so many times that the material was getting frayed from being picked at so. Eventually my teacher looked at it and pointed out to me that the pattern showed making the pleats on the outside of the skirt, rather than the inside. I had never heard of pleats on the outside of a skirt, but I redid them. They looked better, except for the frayed places where the threads had been picked out. The skirt looked awful and I was so embarrassed. But that sweet lady gave me an A on that project, saying that I deserved it for patience. To me that exemplified her whole outlook on life, and she was a pleasure to have as a teacher.

Today, over 60 years later, Edna Ruth Goodner Strickland is in my Sunday School class and I consider her a dear friend, as do most if not all her former students. She has been a constant presence in my life since my sophomore year in high school. I wish all my teachers had been just like her.

I Won What?

When we were sophomores, some teacher assigned us the task of writing an essay on the state of Oklahoma. I didn't have a lot of enthusiasm for the job, and by Sunday afternoon I still hadn't started it, although it was due the next day. Instead, I went roller skating on the Methodist tennis court. I was feeling really good about my skating ability, and about the time I decided I should go professional, I got my come-uppance, so to speak. My wheels hit a crack and I became airborne. What goes up must come down. Suffice it to say that when I got home, I wrote my essay standing up. I turned it in the next day and forgot about it.

Later, I was aware that it had never been returned to me, but assumed it was just an oversight and I had no desire to see it again anyway. Months later, we were in assembly one day when the principal announced that a Heavener student had won first prize in a state essay contest. I was impressed. Wonder who it was? As I sat swiveling my neck trying to locate the lucky writer, I heard my name called. Huh? I hadn't entered any contest. But I numbly walked up on the stage to receive my blue ribbon. I never heard anything more about it and was too embarrassed to ask. I could only assume that the teacher who had assigned the task of writing the essays on Oklahoma must have entered mine in that contest. I sure would like to know what I wrote.

Mr. Winton

Something ran through my mind earlier about our sophomore biology class, and more memories came rushing back. I don't know why that class would be any different from any others, but to me it was. Maybe it was because of the teacher. Maybe it was just at a time in our lives when we were expected to learn more about taking on adult responsibilities.

Mr. Winton was one who caused you to think and plan ahead. I don't think I realized that I was one to procrastinate till that class came along. At the first of school he told us that we would need to gather an insect collection at some unnamed time in the future. He didn't point out that bugs tend to disappear when cold weather comes, and I guess few if any of us were farsighted enough to realize that.

Speaking strictly for myself, I sort of forgot about the insect collection till one day after the weather turned cold and Mr. Winton announced out of the clear blue that our collection would be due in one week. I did notice, however, that I wasn't the only one scrambling around looking for bugs.

I went to the country and started turning over rocks, looking for anything living beneath them. One of the girls was taking down light fixtures, picking out parts of bugs long deceased and gluing them together to make a whole new species. I'm sure she made up names for them as well. I never knew if the teacher bought it.

One memorable challenge Mr. Winton presented to us was dissecting a frog. One of the boys was doing quite well till he realized it was not a plastic model he was working on, but the real thing. They really did have the look and feel of plastic. But not the smell. Sometimes I imagine I can still smell the formaldehyde and it's as sickening as ever. I never really saw the point in that activity. It was certainly the last frog I ever cut up.

One thing that stands out in my mind is that of one of the girls, who was wearing so many can-cans that her skirt stuck almost straight out, making a mad dash down the hall and into the room which was a straight shot at the end of the hall. She was trying to get in the door before the tardy bell quit ringing. She threw on her brakes just inside the door, slid a few feet, then fell flat on her can-cans. The teacher calmly walked over and offered her a hand up, which she accepted with more grace than I could have done.

One thing that happened in that class makes me feel a bit guilty, though. We were supposed to draw a picture of a skeleton on a sheet of poster board and label all the bones. I was still working on it at the last minute, of course. I was never any good at drawing anything without a really good model and even then I always messed it up.

I'm not sure if we were supposed to start at the head or the feet, but I started at the head, and had nothing but a big blob of erasures when my neighbor and classmate, Paulann Johnston came by. She saw how I was struggling and offered to draw the skull for me. I turned the poster board over and gladly accepted her offer of help. She did a beautiful job on the skull and I drew the rest. What could be so hard about drawing the other bones? The only problem was that by the time I got down to the knees, I ran out of space. My skeleton had obviously been a very tall person.

Fearing it might not be acceptable to the teacher, but unable to come up with a better solution, I spliced another sheet of poster board to the bottom, finished out the skeleton, and cut off the excess.

I had a lot of erasures which looked quite messy, so I took a pen with turquoise ink in it and traced over the pencil lines. The finished product didn't look that bad. In fact, the teacher was quite impressed with it, gave me an A, and kept it to display in the room as a model skeleton.

I felt really bad about it, as it had been a series of purely accidental occurrences that produced an acceptable drawing. And it would never have happened without Paulann's help. I don't remember if I ever even thanked her for it. If not, I'd like to do so now.

Thank you, Paulann. Your help was greatly appreciated.

I think that year was the first year of teaching for Mr. Winton. I don't know if we were too hard on him or why he left so soon. As I recall, he was there only that one year. I've often wondered what became of him.

The Throne on the Fountain

At our school, good old Heavener High, there was a fountain out front that had been there for decades and no one I knew had ever seen it wet except when it rained. There was talk of removing it, but no one really wanted to do that. So it just sat there. It was the butt of many jokes. One day we arrived at school to see that someone had performed an amazing feat by putting a toilet commode on the very top of our big round rock fountain. Everybody just looked at it and wondered who could have done it, and went about their business.

Later, in our Senior English class, the teacher left the room for a minute to run an errand. Some of the more creative boys in the class decided to harass her a little. One held the door shut, while another played lookout by watching the hall through the transom over the door, as two of the boys held him up there. He was supposed to announce her return so the one holding the door shut could be fully prepared. Suddenly the watcher yelled, "Hogan!" The others dropped him in the floor and scurried to their seats. The principal (Mr. Hogan) came through the door in time to see the pranksters slide into their seats and we all feared the worst.

Surprisingly, he named three or four of the boys (the ones who had been at the door) and told them he needed them to help him with a job. He said someone had put a commode on the fountain the night before and he needed help to get it down. They meekly left with him and did the job he requested they do. After they left, someone told the rest of the class that the boys he had called to remove the commode were the ones who had put it up there. That was the last I ever heard of it, but we were all amused at the principal's creative way of handling the problem. The boys knew they had been found out, but no big deal was made of what they had done. That must have taken some of the fun out of their prank.

Funny Girl Ann

When we started the ninth grade, I was pleased to learn that we had a lot of new class members who had attended school through the eighth grade in small towns south of Heavener. Now they had come to Heavener to attend high school and teach us new ways of doing things.

One of them was Ann Pledger. I can't remember ever having seen her before then. Later I would learn that she was famous—her picture having been featured on the front of some publication whose name escapes me.

I thought Ann was a pretty blonde girl, but the thing that impressed me most about her was her sense of humor. There was never a dull moment with her around. And that still holds true. I've never seen her in a bad mood.

I can remember attending church camp with Ann. After an excruciatingly long worship service spent sitting on hard wooden pews, she pulled herself to her feet and groaned, "I think if the preacher had said for anybody who wanted to go to hell to stand up, I'd have been the first one on my feet."

Ann may kill me for this, but it was so cute I just have to tell it.

Miss Decker, who taught us typing, shorthand, and bookkeeping, told us that she had boarded with Ann's family while she taught school in the area where Ann lived when Ann was just a tiny girl. Her pet name for Ann was "Droopy Drawers." One day Ann was sitting up near the front of the church before the worship service started and was turned around looking back towards the door. Miss Decker walked in and Ann called loudly, "Hi Dwoopy Dwawers!"

Ann was voted "wittiest girl" in our Senior Who's Who. That was a good call. So far as I can tell, she hasn't changed in that respect. She's always a pleasure to be around and still full of surprises.

She not only has a great sense of humor but is a very kind person. I can't remember ever having heard her say a disparaging word against anybody.

She married Bobby Ray Kirksey a few years after graduation. I don't know Bob very well, but I hope he knows how lucky he is. He is also a very good man. They had a boy and a girl, Craig and Shelly, who have given her five beautiful granddaughters and a grandson. And now she has great-grandchildren as well. She's a wonderful mother and grandmother.

A couple of years ago, Ann and Bob lost their son, Craig, to cancer. Her heart was broken, but she handled it as she does everything. With grace and patience. I'm so blessed to have a friend like Ann.

The Junior Play

I've never been known as a good actress. But when it was time for our Junior play, I tried out for a part that I felt might work for me. There was no way I would have tried out for a leading lady part or anything of that nature. But there was a part for a colored wash lady named Asma and I thought I might handle that. One of my best friends (Ann) tried out for the same part. When the day came to look on the bulletin board to see who was chosen for the parts, my name was not on the list. I had no bad feelings about it and was prepared to congratulate my friend who had been chosen for it. But I didn't get a chance to do that that day. Someone walked up and said that Ann had lost her dad the night before. As I recall he had had a heart attack. My first thought was that I had so much rather get to keep my daddy than to win a part in a school play. My heart broke for her. I was told that while I did not get a part, I was to be the "student director." My sister Norma was the same thing in her Junior play, only back then they had called it the "prompter." I guess someone later decided that "student director" sounded a little more important. In any case, I tried to do what I was told my job was, to help the actors out if they forgot a line. But I became a little more involved than that.

Near the last of the play, the parents of a teenager were sitting discussing something that was going on with their daughter and a friend or two. Seems to me there was some smooching (pardon me—signs of affection) going on onstage at the very end and the maid was to come out and say, "Don't look like nobody here needs a wash lady." The only problem was that Asma had forgotten that she still had that one last line, and had gone to the change room and started getting changed. The couple sitting on the stage were looking rather puzzled since Asma had not come back, so I got their attention and said, in the loudest whisper possible, "AD LIB." Then I rushed to find our errant Asma. The two who were told to ad lib, Glen Lazalier and Alma Brazill, carried on like they had been doing it all their lives. Apparently no one even noticed the brief pause and casual conversation that took place while Asma was getting her gloves back on and rushing back onstage. I felt they should have had an Oscar for their performance. All three of them.

Two Boys Too Many

I didn't date a lot in high school. I had one good friend who was a boy, and he would sometimes walk me home from evening school functions, but he didn't always have access to a car. So we almost never went anywhere except for that. When I was a junior, a good friend of mine was dating a boy who was also a good friend of mine, and he had another friend with whom I became acquainted. We started dating and sometimes double dated. But usually our dates consisted of going to a local movie and straight home, per my parents' instructions. He never complained and was always very polite. I had never really been around boys with impressive manners before, so he was a novelty in more ways than one.

One night when we left the theater, instead of turning right and heading for my house, he turned left as if to circle the block. I didn't think it was a huge deal and thought little of it till he drove a couple of blocks off the main drag and I saw a couple of boys come out of the shadows and approach the street. My friend pulled the car across the almost deserted street and stopped on the other side. The boys walked up to the car, he rolled his window down, and they talked for a few minutes. Nothing but common conversation.

I knew the boys and thought they were good guys. And they may have been. I never really came to know much about them. All I know is what happened in the next couple of minutes. One of them suddenly yanked the driver's door open, slid in, and shoved him over, putting himself in the driver's seat. The other ran around the front of the car and as he approached my door, I pushed down the door lock (it was a two-door car), turned around to put my feet against the door and my back against my friend, and pushed hard enough to eject the boy in the driver's seat. Then I told my friend to get out of there NOW! And he did.

I didn't know then and never found out if he had known that was going to happen or if he was as surprised as I was. I only knew that whether or not anything unseemly happened, my folks would kill me if they ever heard of me being in a car with three boys. I had heard of a couple of local girls who had found themselves in a similar situation and the boys (other boys) had "roughed them up" before releasing them. Strangely, I didn't think much about what had happened, never told a soul for years, and actually went out with him a couple more times before he dumped me for a skinny blonde.

Special Delivery Husband

Growing up, I swear I never had any ambitions to be anything but a wife and mother. I had been blessed with the ability to make pretty good grades in school and several of my teachers had suggestions as to what I should do career-wise. But I never wanted to do anything but marry a good man and have kids. I knew enough to know that a housewife works as hard as anyone in any job, if she does all the things she needs to do. And I was never lazy. But I just didn't know of anything I would rather do. In fact, I started about the time I hit my teens praying for God to send me the man he wanted me to marry.

When I was growing up, there was a joke going around about a girl whose soldier boyfriend was stationed overseas. They exchanged letters every day, and after a year of this, she married her postman.

When I was in high school, I was writing a boy I had met while visiting my cousins in Arkansas. I always cleaned house on Saturdays and often was shaking out rugs or sweeping the porch when the postman came by. He was our neighbor across the street and I had known him most of my life, so it was just natural for me to visit with him if he came by with the mail while I was outside.

So when a college boy became his Saturday substitute, it seemed only natural to visit with him as well, if the timing worked out to do so. On Saturdays I often had a letter to the Arkansas boy ready to mail when the substitute came by. At first I wasn't interested in him, but I wasn't serious about the other boy, and didn't know if I would ever even see him again.

Eventually the substitute postman asked me out and we started dating on a regular basis. It was not love at first sight for either of us. In fact, I was really miserable the first few times I went out with him. One night while I was dressing for a date my mother said, "It looks like you're getting ready to go to a funeral instead of on a date. What's the problem?"

I said, "Well, he's a really nice guy, but he's so serious and I just don't know how to act around him." There was always a lot of joking and teasing going on around our house, and he just didn't seem to be one who would go for that. At that point my mother gave me a bit of advice that I'll never forget. "If you can't be yourself around him, you don't need to be going with him."

So that night I cut loose with all the foolishness that had been struggling to get out every time I saw him. At first his face registered shock, but soon he got in the game and I learned he was really witty and wonderful.

Meanwhile he started working at another part-time job in a grocery store in addition to his Post Office job, and decided not to pursue his goal of becoming an aeronautical engineer. He had been in college majoring in aeronautical engineering for a couple of years at this point. He finally realized that to work in that field, he would have to move to a large city, and he had the country in his veins. He would just hang on to his Post Office connection and hope it would eventually become a regular job.

In January I ruined a knee playing basketball, and he was at my house every day doing anything he could to soothe my pain and help me in any way he could. His kind and caring presence was a great comfort to me and I realized it would be good to have him around forever. He proposed a few days later.

Clem Lee Burroughs and I married three days after I graduated from high school in 1959 . His part-time Post Office job became full time within a few years, and as he plodded through the rain, snow, sleet, and extreme Oklahoma heat, he made a comfortable living for us for 35 years, until he retired from the Post Office, and even after that.

Wearing the white sheath dress my mother had made for me, and the corsage Clem had bought for me, I waited for him to pick me up and drive me to our church across town. It was approaching 8:00 a.m. on Sunday morning, May 24, 1959, and we were about to commit our lives to each other. My sister Inella, her husband, and our little brother, Rick, were there as witnesses. Bro. Gaskin came across the street from the parsonage and performed the ceremony. I suppose I was in a state of shock, as I seem to be so often, because I remember nothing at all about the vows we said. There was no music, no flowers, other than the white carnations in my corsage, and no people there to watch us tie the knot, aside from my little brother, my sister, and her husband. Neither of us wanted anything but to do the deed and get on with our lives. We didn't even kiss after Bro. Gaskin did the "you may kiss the bride" thing. We just hugged and blushed. We were very private people.

We left immediately and drove his old blue Ford up to Roaring River State Park in Missouri, where we spent three nights in a cabin, although the $5 a night it cost for the cabin must have been a hardship on Clem. We had a wonderful time, riding the paddle boats on the lake, which has since been drained and turned into a campground, riding horses from the riding stable, hiking through the hills, and often just lying in bed listening to the rain on the roof.

We had every expectation of driving home and moving in with my folks till we could make arrangements for a place to live, as my older brother and two sisters had done before me. That's all I had ever seen and I just thought it was the way it was done. And Clem was as naïve about it as I was. We had been engaged for several months but had made no big deal of it, no announcement in the Heavener Ledger. We just assumed things were going to work out. And they did. What is the old saying—"God looks out for fools and babies?"

When I had called home to tell my folks that we had arrived at our destination safely, Mother had already been at work fixing things. She asked if we would like to stay in my brother's rented house for a few weeks till we could get things together. He and his wife had a house in town rented and had kept it while they were gone on a pipeline job. It was equipped with everything we could possibly need. Mother said she would call and ask them about it if we liked. We liked. So we moved into a nice enough house and stayed for a few weeks while we prepared a downtown apartment over Otasco for ourselves. Otasco owners, Coy and Edith Robertson, bought the paint and we painted the walls of the apartment. Our church gave us a really nice and appropriate wedding shower, Mother gave us some quilts, and we were in business. We received virtually everything we needed.

We lived in that apartment for about a year, then moved across town into a small rent house behind a larger house where my friend's parents lived. We lived there about a year. Our daughter was born while we lived there.

It's a Girl!

When I went for a doctor's visit in my eighth month, Clem asked him if he would be allowed to be present for the birth. The doctor must have had some bad experiences in that area, because he went ballistic. "No, you won't be in there! And if you try to come in anyway, I'll call the law!"

Needless to say, that was the last time we went to see that doctor. We started looking for another doctor, and wound up in Mena, Arkansas, about 40 miles south and east of us, "over the mountains and through the woods" as the old song goes. It was a long way to drive to have a baby. But Clem was feeling absolutely desperate. He felt he just had to be in there to be sure I was okay.

We drove to the outskirts of Mena and stopped at a pay phone booth. We opened the phone book and looked for "physicians" and the Lord was smiling down on us. The first doctor listed was Dr. Calvin Austin. Clem called the office and talked to a nice lady who said we should come by and talk to him. His office was only a few blocks from the phone booth we were using. Dr. Austin was a very pleasant and reasonable man and did much to put us at ease. He said the subject of the father being in the delivery room had never come up, but he saw no reason why it wouldn't be permissible. We realized later that he probably hadn't been practicing there for long, as he was quite young and didn't seem completely aware of all the policies of the hospital. When we went back for my first appointment, he said the anesthesiologist had been very unhappy about the idea of the father being present for a birth, and said he would not be in there if Clem was. But Doctor Austin told him that he had given us his word and Clem would be in there if the two of them had to do the job alone. But, he added, if Clem would prefer, he could watch the process through the glass in the door to the wash-up room and would know what was going on. So that was the plan.

When the big day came, things came up in the middle of the night, as they always seem to do. As previously arranged, we called Veachel and woke him up, and he went over and got Daddy's Oldsmobile 88, which was the most reliable vehicle in the family at the time. He drove us down to Mena and we checked into the town's only hotel, which was directly across the street from the train depot. The next morning we walked the couple of blocks to the doctor's office and he said it would be a while before the baby came, but to call him when we thought we needed to go to the hospital. I walked the floor all that day with my back hurting. That was the only pain I had.

Finally Clem called the doctor's house and his wife said he was bowling. We should take a taxi to the hospital and she'd contact him and tell him about it. When I arrived at the hospital, the nurse asked about contractions and I told her I had had none. She said I was having one even as we were speaking. To shorten the story a bit, I'll only say that it was a terribly long night for me, as well as for Clem and our doctor. But I had the advantage of being drugged, and he didn't. He threw up all night. Our 8-pound baby girl was born with a huge hematoma on her head. She was facing up instead of down and by the time the doctor saw me, it was really hard for him to turn her. The first time I saw her, the poor baby looked like she had been in a street brawl. But she stared at me with those navy blue eyes and so much as said, "Don't feel sorry for me. The worst part is over."

Clem didn't look much better. He vowed on the spot that he would never "put you through anything like this again."

Stop That Car!

It was almost four years before he relented, after our doctor kept insisting that we shouldn't raise our daughter alone. I was surprised to hear Clem ask the doctor if, should we decide to have another one, he would be allowed to be in the delivery room. Doctor Austin said that the hospital had relaxed a lot of rules in the last four years and he felt sure he would be able to be in there. Less than a year later we had our son, Jim, with his daddy present, and we all had a much easier time than when Sandy was born.

I give Dr. Austin credit for convincing Clem that we needed to have another child. It's a long story how that came about and I won't take the time to tell it all. I will say that it was a more miserable nine months than I had had with Sandy, but a much easier delivery. We planned to go to Mena again, and left home a few days early in order to be sure we were at Mena when the stork came with his special delivery. We went about a week before my due date, but unlike the first time, this baby came a few days early. I had made arrangements for a family member to drive to Mena and pick up Sandy when I went to the hospital, and had a backup plan in place in case her baby brother came early.

So we started towards Mena and a little past Page we saw numerous vehicles parked along the highway on both sides. We asked someone there what was going on and learned that there had been an accident, and several train cars on the tracks down the hill from the road had been derailed. Being a passenger train, it was much more serious than when a freight train derails. Clem parked on the right side of the road and he and Sandy crossed the road and went down the hill to look the situation over. I chose to walk across the road and stand on the down side on the chance of seeing something myself. I was standing actually in the edge of the northbound lane of the road when I heard a man's voice yelling, "Stop that car!" I looked up and saw a green Chevy sedan rolling down the edge of the road towards me, and heard gravel crunching under its tires. Three old men were running after the car but had no hopes of catching it. A short distance to my left was a railroad truck parked on my side of the road. Beyond it and down the hill were my husband and daughter, in addition to many others. I had a hard decision to make because I was the only person around close enough to stop the car. I could see it hitting that big truck, deflecting off it, and rolling down the hill where it would be likely to hit someone. But I was "great with child" and afraid of injuring that child. Suddenly the car was beside me, and I stepped back to let it pass by. Almost without any conscious thought, I reached out, jerked the door open, trotted a few steps, and clumsily climbed into the driver's seat. I was finally able, at the last second, to get on the brakes and stop the car. By then it was moving fast enough to cause the tires to skid in the gravel. The old men came running up, opened the driver's door, and one said, "What a friend!" He was the owner of the car and he was from Heavener. I knew him and his family.

I climbed out of the car, shaking like a leaf, and retreated to my own car across the road, where my husband and daughter soon joined me. We used to hear people talk about "marking" a child by some incident that happened prior to its birth. I was a bit concerned about what effect my adventure might have on my baby, but the only evidence that that might have happened was when my son's first career interest turned out to be as "a race car driver."

A Mother at the Age of Four

We feel that we were greatly blessed with our two children from the start. We had explained to Sandy about the coming baby not long before Jim arrived. She immediately assumed we were getting that baby for her and she had every intention of raising him right. He caught an infection in the hospital, which caused a rash and an eye infection. We were sent home with eye drops to be used periodically, and a chlorophyll wash to be used on his skin daily. Our old house was so cold that I used to sit in a chair in front of the open heater and bathe him on my lap. Putting in the eye drops was a two-person job. Jim naturally hated having drops put in his eyes and made no secret of that fact. If I tried to do it by myself, Sandy would come flying into the mix screaming, "You're hurting my baby!" and doing her best to make me stop. She was always such a good little girl, but she would have fought a tiger for "her baby." Clem had to hold her while I did the dastardly deed. It was such a relief when we finally got past that chore.

A friend, Jo Milligan, had given me a Dr. Spock baby book when Sandy was born and I was inclined to think that Jim must have absorbed the contents of that book even before he was born.

He had conditions I had never heard of. One of his first was "thrush" which was a new one to me. The book told me what it was and how to treat it. We had to paint the inside of his mouth with gentian violet, which of course left his lips purple. He had constant ear infections, colds, and many other problems. When he was four months old, I realized that his feet were crooked. So crooked that I couldn't get a shoe on him. He was referred to a specialist in Fort Smith who put both legs in casts. These had to be changed midway through the process, and the tech who cut the first ones off, cut his legs as well.

When the casts came off for good, he graduated to "Buster Brown splints" which consisted of special shoes that laced all the way up the top of his feet and big bolts with bigger nuts on the bottom end of them, which fastened to a flat bar that held his feet apart and his toes turned out. It must have been so uncomfortable to wear. In order to try to take a step, he had to swing his whole body. Even so, by the time he was about eight months old, he was able to unlatch a window screen and swing the screen out, then back his little body, even with the contraption on his feet and legs, out the window preparatory to dropping to the ground. I caught him just in time to thwart his plans. When he decided to tear the lower corner of the screen off the front screen door and crawl through the hole, I knew it only in time to go out and pick him up off the ground. Fortunately he wasn't hurt, but I was. When he was nine months old, he was trying to walk, although it meant swinging his body around with the bolts on the bottoms of his shoes acting as pivots. So at that point, the doctor gave permission for him to go without the splint in the daytime, which made my life a lot easier.

Before Jim walked and for a while afterwards, I had no clothes dryer and thus had to hang clothes to dry on clotheslines outside.

I really dreaded cold weather when the clothes would freeze to the lines. Sandy was a lifesaver as far as her brother was concerned. He really hated it when I went out and left him and would scream at the top of his voice. One day I planted him in the middle of the kitchen floor, told Sandy to watch him and not let him out of her sight, and I would be back as soon as I possibly could. I had barely left the house and hung a few clothes when the screaming stopped. That concerned me so I retreated to the house to check on them. Sandy had a jar of peanut butter and a spoon and was shoveling it into his mouth. I said, "Oh no! He might choke on that. He's still a little too small for peanut butter."

She said, "Why? He's eating it. He likes it. He's not crying anymore." He wasn't crying, because he couldn't get his mouth open. But she did her best.

The poor little guy learned to walk before his first birthday in spite of the difficulties. When he was four, he had a tonsillectomy and tubes put in his ears. It has been one thing after another for his whole life.

Prayer for Rain Answered

When Jim was about four, we were in the middle of a terrible drought. Driving home from Poteau, I remarked that it looked like Monroe (a few miles to our east) was getting some rain, and sure wished we were. Jim looked at me like he was completely puzzled and said, "Well all you have to do is ask God and He'll give us some rain." I felt embarrassed and humbled and said, "You're right. Will you ask Him, too?"

He said, "I already did."

The next morning when we got up, it was raining. When Jim got up and came in the kitchen, I said, "Look outside. It's raining."

He shrugged his little shoulders and said, "I knew it would be."

Growing up, everything seemed easy for Sandy. I wish we had been in a time and place where she could have had training in gymnastics. But at the time, there was nothing like that around here. Her daddy built her a trapeze which hung from a tree out back by the barn. It wasn't unusual to see her hanging by one foot and then somehow flip off and land on her feet. Even as a toddler, she did tricks on her tricycle, pedaling it through the house as fast as she could, then slamming her feet down on the floor just short of the kitchen door. She turned the handlebars around and sat on them that way, and did tricks on the swings on the swing set and even the tire swing. She never cared much for softball or basketball, although she seemed to have a knack for them both. When her brother was less than school age, he talked her into playing softball with him one day, and she was to bat. He was almost instantly back in the house with his lips already swollen to twice their size. He had pitched a ball for her to bat and she hit the first one he pitched, which went straight to his mouth. She felt so bad about that that she refused to play ball with him again for years.

In the sixth grade, there were more P.E. students than basketball uniforms so the coach had to choose the ones to give them to. He told me that he gave Sandy one and she said she didn't really care that much, to just give the uniform to someone who really wanted one. He complained about that every time he saw me for years. He said she could have been a good player.

Sandy also did well on her schoolwork and graduated as the uncontested valedictorian of her class. Years later when she decided to become a court reporter, she made it though the training in less time than any student who had gone through the training there had ever done.

In short, everything she has ever tried has seemed to come easy for her.

She learned to sew when she was about 13. I don't remember teaching her and she was too young for home ec at school, but she learned it. One day when I was working out in the cake shop, she came out and asked me how I planned to make the dress I had bought material for weeks before. I just told her I thought I'd make it like the blue one I had made a while back. I never even wondered why she asked because I was up to my eyeballs in cake icing and running behind. So she went back to the house and I thought nothing more about it. When I went in the house a few hours later, there was a beautiful new red dress, completely finished, even to the hem, hanging on my bedroom door. She had found the pattern and made the dress, hemming it according to the one I had made earlier.

I'm sure a lot of things must have been hard on her, but she just never complained. Not even when she was going through cancer surgery and chemotherapy a few years later.

Not so for Jim. He always had a struggle in everything. He was a good baseball player and did well at basketball, but he always gave everything his all. He had a hard time learning to talk. He tried so hard but it took him such a long time to get past his difficulties. We took him to McAlester to have him tested at a clinic over there and they said the messages between his mind and his mouth were getting scrambled before they reached his mouth. They gave him fine motor control exercises to do which were to straighten out the signals. He was to walk a balance beam, which could be just a plank on the floor. We tried that and it got old in a hurry. So his daddy took him out to the railroad, which was conveniently close to our house, and they spent hours walking the rails. That was great fun for him. We bought him several of the little hand-held games that were popular back then—basketball, baseball, etc.—and he mastered them fast. When the Pac Man game came out, he decided to stay up one night and see how high he could go in it. He made it past 3 million and Pac Man just sort of gave up and quit trying. A few years later, his baseball coach, who had played professionally, said he had the fastest hands he had ever seen. (Recently Jim told me that his sister had given him a new one of those little games for his birthday in February.)

After a few trips to McAlester for speech therapy, his therapist started coming to our local school to help those in the lower grades who were having problems. Although he wasn't quite old enough for kindergarten, we were allowed to take him over there rather than having to drive to McAlester. He was doing well when his therapist said she would be leaving. Her husband was coming home from Vietnam and they would be moving away. She said she thought it best that Jim not have any more therapy till after he started to kindergarten because he was trying so hard it wasn't good for him. Plus, she thought he'd learn faster when he started being around other kids. And that was true. By the time he finished kindergarten, he could talk as well as any of his classmates.

Postscript to that story. Now Jim is a regional supervisor with the fisheries division of the Oklahoma Dept. of Wildlife, and they fly him all over the country to make presentations to large groups, about programs involving fish and the environment, some of which he started and has been involved in for years. He has a bachelor's degree in biology and a masters in Environmental Science. It still amazes me to think of that little boy struggling to be understood and see where he is today.

He also amazes me with all the things he can do. He was never a quitter but sometimes I find it hard to realize that the little guy who had such a hard time has learned to do so many things. In 2018, his house flooded to the eaves. While some others just walked off and left the bank to deal with it, he felt that would not be the honorable thing to do, so he set in and rebuilt the house from the ground up. He rented a jackhammer and broke up the entire floor, which already had problems before the flood, hauled the concrete outside a bucket at a time, and disposed of it. While he never liked working on a house, he rebuilt that house from the ground up. Many people were good to him, giving him some money here and there and volunteering to do jobs that he could not do alone. His son-in-law's friend owns a dry wall company in

Chickasha and he brought up a crew and completely sheet-rocked that house and would take no pay for their labor. That was an amazing gift! As is par for the course with him, every imaginable thing went wrong with that job but he just hung in there till it was finished and he was finally able to sell it for enough to pay it off.

2009—Not A Good Year

2009 was a hard year for our family. Sandy had breast cancer and Jim was bitten by a copperhead. I had my second hip replacement that year as well. But God was merciful and brought us all through it.

The Mail Route

Clem made a lot of friends on his mail route, helped many people, and was very conscientious about it all. Some people became almost like family to him. He had no place to take a break on the far west side of his route, and an older couple became aware of it. They started asking him in for coffee and pie (and the restroom) and great conversation. He came to think more of Virg Story and his sweet wife, Bess, than just about anyone he knew. He was a very old man who still made a big garden, and Clem worried about interrupting his work in the garden. But Virg just shook off his protests and insisted that he come in.

Virg had a little cocker spaniel named Jiggs and Jiggs usually had a story to tell as well. One day when Clem arrived at their house, there was a pile of cantaloupes by the front door. Virg asked Clem if he wanted to buy one, because Jiggs was having a cantaloupe sale. Jiggs had picked them and dragged them to the house. He also liked to eat them. One day Virg told Clem that they had had a baptizing at their house that morning. It had rained and a small ditch in the yard was full of water. Jiggs had taken the family cat by the scruff of the neck to the ditch and ducked him under the water.

One of his favorite stories was about how that morning he had gotten up first, and Bess asked him to bring her a glass of water. She had gone back to sleep and forgotten about it when he brought her the water. She asked what that was all about and he told her she had asked for a drink of water. She had no memory of it and said she didn't want any water. So he poured it on her. The next morning when Virg woke up, Bess was standing by the bed holding a glass of water. He asked her what she was doing. She said, "Here's your drink of water."

He said, "Water? I don't want… Thank you!" So he drank the water.

One day while Bess was getting Clem a piece of pie, Virg warned him that she had used frozen crusts and had failed to take the paper out from between them before she baked the pie. She was almost blind.

One time when Bess was in the hospital, I decided to bake two coconut cream pies, one for Clem and one to take to Virg. I couldn't find my usual recipe so made them from a different recipe. They tasted too sweet to me, but I thought since Clem likes things sweet, it wouldn't bother him. I took one across town and gave it to Virg, telling him not to tell Clem that I had made it. So at noon Clem came home, looking a little weak, and said he didn't want any lunch. He said, "Virg had made a coconut pie and brought me a huge piece of it. It was so sweet it made me sick, but I didn't want to hurt his feelings, so I just ate it." I just walked over to the cabinet, picked up the second pie, walked outside to the back gate and dumped the pie out. Clem was in shock, absolute disbelief.

He asked why I had done that and I said, "It's a mate to the one you ate at Virg's."

His Post Office job had been so wonderful when he first went to work, but the management in Tulsa had the say over how things were done in this tiny town over a hundred miles away. And they made it as hard on him, on everyone below them, as possible. So he vowed to retire at the earliest possible opportunity.

When he was six months short of his 55th birthday, when he had hoped to retire, the management (higher up than Tulsa) offered an early out for anyone within six months of 55. And they even offered to pay anyone willing to accept that offer, for six months of work, just as if they were still on the job. Needless to say, he jumped at that chance.

Ten months after he retired from the Post Office, he went to work for the Heavener school system as assistant technology director. He had studied computers since the first home computers had become available, hoping that the day might come when he could find work in that field after retiring from the Post Office. He paid in no retirement to the school, knowing he'd have to work for 10 years to qualify for any retirement, and he was sure he would not be there that long. He worked at that job for 14 years and loved every minute of it. He felt that the people he worked for and with at the school were a breath of fresh air after dealing with the politics of the Post Office management. He hated to leave that job and the people he worked with at the school, but was 70 years old and still wanted to get in some traveling while he still felt like it. So he reluctantly left the best job he had ever had.

Daddy

My father, Earl Leslie Hiram Linville, was born in Arkansas on June 18, 1909 to William Boone Linville and Lou Alice Babbitt Linville. We only recently realized that William Boone was probably named after the William Linville whose nephew was Daniel Boone.

Daddy had an older brother, Carl, and 10 years down the road would have a half-brother. His dad died when Daddy was four and his mother struggled to make it alone. She later married a McBride and had a son by him, Vernie Westman McBride. Daddy was apparently named after two uncles, Earl and Hiram Babbitt. I have no idea where the Leslie came from. His mother and the McBride divorced when Vernie was about three years old.

I never got to see much of Vernie and his family till after my parents died. I remember seeing him a few times and his mother twice before my parents were gone. Somewhere in the mid-to-late 80's, Clem and I made a trip to California, where Vernie had lived for decades, and on a whim I looked in a phone book and found a phone number and address for him in Crescent City. So I called him up and then we found them and visited for a while. We went back to see them a number of times before he died at the age of 95. His wife, Rachel, was living when we went for a number of those visits, but she passed away first.

For a number of years, I called Vernie several times a week and he told me things about the family that I had not heard before. Daddy just never talked much about family. Vernie said he remembered vividly when his dad had left. He said, "Him and Mama got in a big fight and he just walked out and never came back." I'm sure he never paid a dime of child support so that was another mouth for his mother and brother (Daddy) to feed. He said his dad came back to the area and stayed for a while after a few years. He said that once he was walking down the road and his dad was sitting on a porch talking to another man. "He called me over and gave me 50 cents. It was the first money I had ever had. I thought of all I could do with it, but knew I had to give it to Mama and Earl to buy food."

He said a few years down the road he saw his dad trying to unload a wagon that he assumed he was getting paid to do. His dad had called him over and said, "Son, would you do this for me? I just can't do it." He did it and it was the last time he ever saw his dad, who died a few days later.

I had been told that Daddy was put to work in the cotton patch when he was four years old, and that at the age of 13, he was cooking for a road construction crew. Vernie told me that when Daddy was about 16, he was making hamburgers for a man who had a "stand" at a fair. Vernie was standing around watching, and said he was so hungry he could have died. I asked him why he didn't ask Daddy to make him a hamburger and he said he knew if he did, Daddy would have to pay for it and that it would be taken out of his pay. It took every cent Daddy could rake up to put any food on the table. I assume that Uncle Carl had married and moved out by then.

Vernie said when Daddy was about 18, he was able to buy a very old Model A car, and he took out the rumble seat and put a small truck bed in its place. He said it would haul half a rick of wood each load. Daddy was selling firewood for $1 a rick, and making two trips to Muse to deliver a rick. I'm assuming they were living out in the country from Muse at the time. He must have made a little money because Vernie said Daddy bought him the first Christmas present he had ever had that year. Vernie would have been about eight. He said, "Earl got me a cap pistol and a "French harp"and I thought it was so great. I put the French harp to my lips to blow on it and it froze to my lips, because our old house was so cold." He said Daddy was always so good to him—his other brother not so much.

Mother

Mother, Allie Adele Turner Linville was born at Kirby, AR on July 26, 1910 and lived there till she married Daddy at the age of 19. Daddy was 20 and they married at the depth of the Great Depression in 1929. It hurts me to think of how little they had to get by on.

Mother came down with typhoid on their first anniversary. At the time, they were sharecropping, and I hope by then the crops had been harvested, because Daddy would have had no opportunity to get them in after she fell sick. The raging fever was sapping the very life from her and there was nothing to be done. Daddy made a straw mattress and put it out on the porch. When her fever would spike, he would carry her out and put her on that mattress, then draw buckets of water and pour over her. He said the local doctor in the area came to their house every day for six weeks, knowing there wouldn't be a cent of pay for him. Many people were in the same condition during the Depression.

Mother was a tall, big-boned woman who usually carried a good deal of weight. She said that when she finally recovered from the typhoid, she weighed 116 pounds. She also miscarried the baby that would have been born within a couple of months under normal conditions. She had little memory of the last six weeks.

They had a life of hard work and little else. They were married for 65 years, but unfortunately, Mother had Alzheimer's for a number of years before she died at the age of 84. Daddy was in terrible pain from rheumatoid arthritis but lived to be 87 years old.

They had six children born alive and outlived two of them. They were good people, good parents and grandparents, and good neighbors. Either of them would do anything they could to help anyone else. I remember a poor old ragged man coming to their door one time after all of us were grown and gone. In those days it wasn't uncommon for hoboes to knock on your door and ask for food. All this man asked for was to use her bathroom. She said he appeared to be almost blind as well as old and sickly. She told him to "go on back in there where you see the light" and then she went outside till he came out. Then she not only fed him but since my older brother was there at the time, she asked him to get a long men's coat (I never had any idea where it had come from) and put on the man. He had appeared to be so cold. The man seemed very grateful, ate his food, and left. I never really thought of it at the time, but I have to wonder if that man might have been an angel in disguise.

My dad, as long as he could get around at all, hobbled around the neighborhood every morning to check up on his neighbors that he considered to be in worse shape than he was. He was crippled up with rheumatoid arthritis that had been working on him since he was in his early 50's. By the time he became bedfast, he had outlived most of his friends and older neighbors so he had few visitors.

Clem's Folks and the Old House

The first time it rained at night after we moved into the old house, we had to get up and move the bed over. It was raining in our faces. Although Clem had lived in that house from 1956 when his family moved into it till 1959 when we got married, he apparently was unaware that the roof leaked. And as it turned out, there must have been a lot of things he was unaware of.

His parents had a unique sleeping arrangement, which could have explained the fact that he didn't know a lot about the old house. The first time he took me to his parents' house, I had a bit of a problem figuring out what was going on. The four of us sat in the living room where the heater lived and visited a while. Then his dad said, "I think it's time for me to go to bed," and he got up and walked out the back door. By this time, his folks were 77 and 65 years old. Like most older folks, they no longer slept in the same room. Only instead of separate bedrooms, they had separate houses. His dad had been a bachelor till the age of 33 and was pretty well used to doing things his own way. He could cook well enough to get by and preferred the privacy of his own house, so when the family moved from Howe to Heavener in 1956, he built a one-room house at the back of the garden and moved his things into it.

Prior to moving to Heavener, they had been caring for both her mother and his step-mother. Her mother stayed in their house with the family and his lived in a small house next door. In order to keep a closer watch on his aging step-mother, he stayed at her house till she passed away and no longer needed him. By that time, he was once again pretty well used to the bachelor life. Her mother also passed away not long afterwards. With the mothers both gone, they decided to move to Heavener. He lived in the little house he built and still did all the usual husbandly things such as taking care of the lawn and repairing things that needed some attention in both the big house out front and his smaller one out back. He also made a big garden. There was no problem between the two; they just liked a little more privacy than most couples.

A few years later, she decided she needed to move closer to town. Neither of them drove, so we drove them to doctors and anywhere else they needed to go. But a few blocks down the street from the old house, there was another big old house for sale and right next door to it was a small grocery store. Her dream was to buy that house so she could just walk next door and buy just about anything she needed. That was not his dream.

I never knew exactly how it came about, but somehow we wound up buying that old house and he stayed in his little house out back. He still went down to her house and mowed the lawn, etc. as he had always done, and walked to town when he needed anything. Clem stopped by his mother's house almost every day to see if she needed anything, and we loved having his dad nearby. It was worth so much to him and to us to have our kids grow up with him living practically in our back yard. I think by the time he passed away at the age of 89, our kids were the only grandchildren he actually remembered. And they adored him. It was sad, but the others lived far enough away to make their visits too infrequent for him to remember.

In his last few years, his short-term memory failed to such an extent that it made it really hard for him to cope. There was a time when one of my friends was visiting and he came to our house, came in and told me something, then started back to his house. Before he got halfway home, he turned around and came back and said, "Did I tell you?????(whatever it was he had just told me.) He was always so hard on himself when he forgot anything and would refer to himself as "Stupid old fool!" and other equally sad things. So I just acted like I hadn't heard that before. I felt sure that my friend, who had heard him tell me that, wondered if my mind was going as well. Especially after he came back for the fourth or fifth time and we repeated the conversation. It would have done him no good to reinforce the negative opinion he already had of himself.

Working on the Old House

One thing I insisted on doing before we moved into that house was to redo the kitchen. Neither of us had any experience with carpenter work, other than the jobs I had helped Daddy with in his house, so it was hard to know where to start. The first thing we had to do, of course, was to hire somebody to replace the roof. There would have been no way we could have done that job ourselves. Although, a few years down the road, I did replace the roof on the back porch by myself while Clem was at work. And the two of us replaced the front porch roof.

The old kitchen cabinets were painted lime green and red, and there was ragged wall paper on the walls and ceiling of that room. The walls were papered in ancient green print with pink flowers on it. The once-white paper on the ceiling hung in tatters that allowed dirt to sift down from the attic. We stripped the paper from all surfaces and started our first attempt at hanging sheetrock. That part wasn't so bad, but we had no idea at all how to go about taping and finishing the sheetrock. I was so happy when my brother, Veachel, came by and showed us how it was done. We painted the cabinets white and the ceiling and upper part of the walls white, with the lower part red. It wasn't perfect, but it could be cleaned. We eventually redid all the rooms in the house, put in new windows and doors, took off siding from the outside and put fiberglass batting in the walls, put the siding back on and covered it with new siding, and eventually bricked the lower half or so of the walls.

The floors were bad, so we had listened to some well-meaning but uninformed person who told us to put particle board down on top of them and new linoleum or tile over that. Then the plumbing job started. Although that house sat no more than a foot off the ground, less in some places, and one might expect wood rot, etc. on the underside of the floor, there actually seemed to be none and no moisture under the house. We might have expected termites as well but saw none of them for many years. Pap had shoveled dirt up around the lower part of the outside walls, and apparently that did what he intended. But we were concerned that if a pipe sprang a leak and got water under the house, we would be in trouble. Many times while we lived out there, there was flooding all around us and we shuddered to think of water getting under the house. But it never did.

We hired a plumber to replace all the pipes in the one bathroom we had at the time, as well as the line that ran to the kitchen. The floor was taken up enough to accommodate him as he worked on it. Right off we knew we had made a mistake. The plumber complained of a terrible headache the first day he came. Instead of going home and coming back later, he tried to do some of the work. He had to come back the next day and do it all over. Eventually when he reached the point of starting on the line to the kitchen, he vowed that the pipe going to the kitchen would never leak "for at least 50 years," and refused to replace it. We didn't believe him, but thought we'd quit while we were ahead. We paid him, way too much for what he little he did, and did over, and he left.

A couple of months later, I went in the bathroom and heard water spraying up on the underside of the floor. Clem cut the water off and tore up the floor boards to check it out. Not only was the pipe to the kitchen broken, but a lake of water stood under most of the house. There was white chunky-looking mold on the underside of the entire floor. A few weeks later, I went in our bedroom and saw a hump in the linoleum behind our bed. I stomped on the hump and my foot went through to the ground. We had to tear out a wall we had put in that large room so one of the kids could have a small room in that area as well, and strip the room. We wound up breaking that floor up with a sledgehammer and shoveling it out the window. The same for every floor in the house. The combination of the particle board, which soaks up moisture like a sponge, and the water under the house, had turned them all to mush. We replaced them all, room by room, with no help from outsiders.

We had trouble with the sewer from the day we moved in. When it rained, the only water you could get out of the house was what you carried out. We had a new septic system put in, one that was supposed to bring water to the surface to evaporate rather than having it "perk" through the soil. It was better but nowhere near what it needed to be. Finally, many years later, the city ran a sewer line up by our house. But it was across the street, so we had to have a line laid across the road to reach the new sewer line. We were so happy. For a short time. Then suddenly we were back to square one. We called in expert help—twice—and finally found out that either the city or the county had cut through our sewer line on the far side of the road, while doing another job. We finally made it through that crisis as well.

While living in the old house, we built a large room in the attic. My dad, of course, wanted to help. I knew he wasn't able to climb those stairs and do that work, but knew it would hurt his feelings if we refused his help. We had no idea how to start, but Daddy figured that out. He was mainly there in the role of consultant, till we were finally able to start some painting up there. We put white paneling on the sloping ceiling, dark paneling on the walls, and painted the trim white. I can't recall why we had dark paint up there, but we were apparently using it for something. Anyway, it was there along with the white.

I shuddered at the thought of Daddy trying to paint, his vision being what it was, but I couldn't stand to hurt his feelings. So I handed him a brush, gulped a couple of times, and walked away. Not long afterwards, I worked up enough nerve to look at his work and it was just as I feared. He was getting white paint on the dark paneling and I just knew it would never come off without taking the finish off the paneling.

When he left to go home for the night, I went up to inspect the damage. It was worse than I had even expected. He had obviously gotten a lot of white paint on the dark paneling and then tried to cover it up with dark paint. I can't remember what all I used, but after several hours I was actually able to get both the white and dark paint off the paneling without damaging the finish. I breathed a sigh of relief and went downstairs to fix a very late supper.

Early the next morning, Daddy was back and went straight upstairs as fast as his crippled old legs would take him. He went up with a look of concern on his face, but came down looking greatly relieved. He told me rather sheepishly, "Yesterday I got some white paint on the dark paneling and thought of covering it up with dark paint. This morning you can't even tell there was a problem with it."

I said, "Really? It looks fine to me."

* * *

When we started to try to build deep shelves in the kitchen to accommodate our computer and all that went with it, Daddy was there to run his ancient table saw and help with the project. The problem was that the saw was old and the blade had also seen better days. His eyes were so far gone that I worried that he might cut off his fingers. The walls in that old house were so crooked that it was almost impossible to keep anything square and straight. I planned to use a furring strip to disguise the fact that the cabinets would not fit in the place we wanted them. The corner where one big unit was to go took such a bend between floor and ceiling that if would have been impossible for even the best carpenter to make a unit to fit exactly in that corner. I went out to hold the sheet of plywood he was about to cut and shuddered when I saw how the warped blade was taking a turn that would guarantee the board would never fit in the intended place. When we finished the job and had a big, heavy unit put together, Clem and I carried it into the kitchen. The cabinet fit the corner absolutely perfectly! No one would ever have been able to make it fit that way intentionally. Daddy was so proud of it and I was, too.

The House that Ed Built

For years we had been talking about building a new house outside the city limits. The man who owned the place where we had bought building materials for 35 years begged us to find a way to move. But Clem refused to "dump our problems on someone else." After we finally got the sewer remedied and a lot of other problems solved, we felt the time was right. He retired from the Post Office and started drawing his retirement, and then went to work for the school in less than a year. I was also working at the church at the same time, so we had the equivalent of three small salaries to work with. After years of looking for the perfect place to build, we lucked into the property we eventually bought to build on, and stayed in the old house till after the house was built and we moved into it. In fact, we let friends who were also trying to build a house stay in the old one after we moved out. Eventually we were ready to sell the old house and the Lord smiled upon us. Some people bought it and seemed glad to get it.

Our new house, which Ed McClain built for us in 1996, was a dream come true. He was such a pleasure to work with and is one of the most honest and agreeable people I've ever met. He worked at saving us money while doing a good job on everything and never gave us a minute of worry about anything.

We had planned to build a small room upstairs to be Clem's "bear's den" but somewhere in the process it grew beyond our wildest dreams. Ed had built a small closet of sorts in the sunroom, which had originally been intended to be just a back porch, planning to put a spiral staircase up to the "bear's den." Somehow I didn't really like the idea of the spiral staircase but didn't know another way to do it. So one day I was looking up through the hole where the staircase was to go and asked Ed if it would be possible to build just a straight stairway above the closet. He did some figuring and said it would. So the original closet built for the spiral stairway became a storage closet in the sunroom that had evolved, and a regular staircase went up. Looking at it later, and seeing the somewhat narrow space left between the staircase and north wall of the upstairs room, I could envision a usable kitchen. We wound up with a small but complete kitchen north of the stairs, with full-sized frig, apartment range, regular double sink, ample cabinets, and a microwave. Upstairs there's also a full-size bathroom with whirlpool tub, an adequate living room and a basic bedroom. We have lived up there for months at a time in cold weather, as the wall-hung heater heats the room in the coldest weather with only the pilot light. The central heat and air don't adequately serve the upstairs, so we put in a window unit that cools it as well as the heater heats it. And that's even better than planned, because anyone staying up there can adjust the temperature independently of the downstairs.

Even better, it's a wonderful place for guests to stay, and has been used for that purpose a number of times. One of my nieces lived up there for nine months in recent years after losing her house to fire and her husband to suicide in four days' time. Friends who had a house fire also stayed up there a couple of months. We feel that small apartment is a special gift given to us to use to help others.

Neighbors on Timber Ridge

One good thing about the location is that when we moved out here, our neighbors across the street were the Chronisters, Eldred, Mary, Mark, and Jeff, who has been our son's best friend since before they started to school. The boys were already grown and gone, but it was always good to see them when they came home for a visit. Eldred was on the school board, and was one who encouraged Clem to apply for the computer job at the school. Both he and Mary were incredibly good neighbors to us till they built a new house farther north and moved.

Scott and Janie Hairrell live next door, and we watched their sons, Jon and Wade growing up. If there were ever any better boys, I've never known of it. Janie was Clem's immediate supervisor when he worked at the school. They are both wonderful neighbors.

Mrs. Walters (Bonita) lived across the street from the Hairrells and was such a good friend. She passed away several years ago and I miss her so much. Her daughter, Georgia, and husband Howard Taylor live in her house now. They are also wonderful neighbors.

Up the road we have Leroy and Bobbie Nolan, for whom I worked a while at their store in the Hembree Chevrolet and

Appliance Center building downtown. When we moved in here, they did all they could to help us get settled. They have been such good friends to us.

Bill and Lynne Pitchford, old friends from church, and the Olivers who are new to the area, also live north of us. Bill and Lynne are prayer warriors and in bad times, it's always good to know that they're praying for all their neighbors. Towards the highway, south, are Midge and Norma Harris, and Dana Scott. Bob Nichols lives in the house on the corner of Timber Ridge and Hwy. 270. While we don't "neighbor" a lot, we know all these people are good people and enjoy having them in such close proximity. We feel safe up here on the hill and would trust any of our neighbors in any situation.

Betty Burns is our nearest neighbor to the south. She and her husband, Norris, moved into the nearly new house vacated by Jim and Leslie Haynes when they had to leave this area for a new job. Sadly, Norris died a couple of years after they moved out here. Betty is like the Energizer Bunny. At the age of 80, she still plays basketball on a women's team which has won many tournaments in many states and walks in marathons or half marathons, winning in her age bracket in almost every case. She has been a good neighbor to us, both out here on Timber Ridge and for years when we both lived out on the Old Pike. For years back in the seventies and eighties, she and I walked five miles every day. Then I took a job and she kept walking. By looking at us, it's not hard to tell which one kept walking.

We are so thankful for our friends and for our home. But we keep reminding ourselves that while we love our home, it's not necessary to our happiness. The Good Lord has taken care of us every day of our lives and our happiness doesn't depend on our material possessions.

Learning to Fly

Clem had intended to go into the Air Force after high school, as his much older brother had done. During his many years in the Air Force, George had flown almost everything, including helicopters.

George never talked a lot about what he did. And we never got to see much of him, as he always seemed to be stationed in distant places. Clem had a lot of respect for him and George had always been one he could count on.

Clem was unable to pass the vision part of the Air Force physical, so that dream was shot down. But it didn't dampen his dream of flying a plane.

He also had the privilege of flying with Mr. Burnett a few times. He was a wonderful, generous man. He owned the local sawmill, which gave a number of people good jobs for many years. And he owned one of the few planes in the county.

One time when Clem had had a tooth pulled, his jaw was badly swollen and he was feeling awful. He was sitting around in his recliner just barely surviving, when Mr. Burnett called and invited him to go flying with him. He would have gone with both legs and both arms broken. A swollen jaw certainly wasn't going to stop him.

Once they flew to Muskogee to Hatbox field. Two of our granddaughters played softball on that field in later years.

For several years, during mowing season, every day after finishing his mail route, Clem came home and repaired lawn mowers, putting aside part of what he earned for flying lessons. Finally, in 1966, he felt his time had come.

He made arrangements to take lessons at the Fort Smith airport, with Pat Casey from Mena as the instructor. Casey was a retired Navy man and had also retired from Real Estate sales. He may have been around for a while, but he was still young at heart.

From the start, Clem struggled with air sickness. That was nothing new for him, but FAA regulations forbid the use of motion sickness drugs while operating a plane. For many days, the two of them left the airport with Casey flying the plane and returned the same way. Clem had spent the entire time in the air hunched over an air sickness bag. He said if he spent all he had saved and accomplished nothing beyond learning to ride in a plane without throwing up, it would be worth the cost.

One day, however, they returned to the terminal building with Clem grinning from ear to ear. He had finally been able to control his air sickness well enough to handle the controls for the first time. But there were white spots--salt deposits-- on the front of his pants legs where the sweat had dripped from his hands.

Clem was making progress, both in his flying ability and in his efforts to control his air sickness, when Casey announced it was time for him to make a cross country flight. Casey wanted him to fly to Mena and Clem asked me to go along. Of course Casey would be there beside him should he encounter a problem.

This was a month or two before our son Jim was born. These

days I'm sure one would be discouraged from riding in a plane in that condition. Especially with Casey in command.

Casey instructed Clem to circle the small terminal building at the Mena airport. As they neared the terminal, Casey suddenly took control of the plane, put it into a power dive right towards the terminal building, then at the last minute, pulled back up sharply. He knew people in the terminal and thought it would be great fun to buzz the place.

As the plane ended its unexpected (for Clem and me) dive and started the sudden climb, Clem lost his last meal, which hit the windshield and splattered on everything in the front seat, including Casey. It served him right. I was thankful to be in the back seat, but didn't feel too stable myself at the moment.

Around 1966 or '67, Roy Reed of Poteau hired an instructor to come to Poteau and teach a ground school to anyone who cared to participate. Clem jumped at it, and wanted me to join him for moral support. My parents kept the kids while we attended the classes.

At the end of the ground school, Reed hired an FAA inspector to come down and give the written test to those who had taken the class. Clem and I had the advantage over the others, as we could study together. We were surprised to learn we had made the two highest scores in the class.

I had always planned to learn to fly, though not necessarily to get a license, but in case Clem should have a heart attack or some such when I flew with him. I seldom flew with him though, as I felt one of us should be left alive to raise our kids. If that indicates I wasn't that comfortable with flying, there's a reason. I wasn't. I thought, though, that once the kids were grown, I would feel better about it.

I even took an hour of actual flying instruction, just to get an idea of what it was like to be in control of a plane. It wasn't a bad experience, as Casey was a wonderful pilot and made everything fun.

About that time we went to the airport at Poteau to hire someone to take my sister and her kids for a plane ride. We knew the manager of the airport, and he thought it would be best for my sister and the kids to ride in the back seat, so he said I'd be welcome to go along for the ride.

As the front seat passenger, I had my own set of controls, and the pilot suggested I put my hands and feet on the controls and "feel how to fly a plane." Because of my hour of flight training, I thought it would be a good experience. It wasn't.

As we started down the runway for takeoff, the plane wobbled from side to side, then suddenly jumped from the tarmac and continued to climb steeply. I thought it was the worst take-off I had ever seen.

"I have a surprise for you," the pilot said. "Were you aware that you made that takeoff?"

That certainly cleared things up. I understood why it had been such a sorry takeoff, but not why he would have taken that risk, especially with my sister and her kids in the plane.

Then he turned towards me and spoke again and the odor of alcohol on his breath explained it all. He said, "You're flying the plane now," and my blood ran cold. We didn't even know he drank. I had no way of knowing how much his judgment was affected at the moment.

I tried to line the plane up with the highway below, as I had heard Clem talk about doing. That was easier said than done. I found myself making a long series of S-turns. I couldn't get used to the fact that planes respond to commands so much more slowly than cars do.

I begged him to take over and he just laughed at me. Every time I thought of having to land the plane, I had trouble breathing. I found myself instinctively pulling back on the yoke and gaining altitude instead of losing it.

I just knew if I tried to land the plane and aimed at the Poteau runway, we would wind up in Poteau River or in the trees on Poteau mountain. If you can't line up with a highway, how would you line up with a runway?

By the time he finally took pity on me and took back control of the plane, I knew I would never be able to put one on the ground in one piece. And I wasn't that thrilled with being a passenger in a plane whose pilot was not completely sober. Especially with family members in the back seat. What must they have been thinking through all this?

My nephew Chris who had been quite small at the time of the plane ride, still says he has never forgotten that flight and has never had any desire to get on a plane again. No wonder the poor kid felt that way.

Clem continued his lessons and eventually earned his private pilot's license. On November 12, 1967, he rented a plane and flew it to the Heavener airport where he gave rides to several friends who had not flown before.

The next day, his brother George was killed in a plane crash in Nevada, where he was being trained to train spotter pilots to drop smoke bombs to direct attacks on targets in Vietnam. He was nine months short of retirement. In spite of that, Clem continued to fly whenever he could afford to rent a plane for an hour or two.

A number of years ago, he suffered occasional blackouts that always happened at night. It was eventually diagnosed as a sudden drop in blood pressure caused from jumping out of bed with a leg cramp. One can't pass the required physical exams if he has had blackouts in the last five years. He hasn't had an exam in years, though it has been over ten years since he had a blackout. So his license is no longer current.

He would still like to fly from time to time, but would be required to be checked out by an inspector, and the cost of plane rental has skyrocketed since then. He has had to choose between flying and traveling, so has chosen to travel instead. And now, at the age of 81, he would be afraid to try to fly again. But the desire to do so is still strong.

Working at the Church

At the time I was hired as secretary of our church, our older and wiser pastor warned me that if I wasn't very careful, I was likely to become cynical from dealing with people who came in off the street looking for a handout. He was right.

There were those who came in often needing groceries, or a utility bill paid, medication, many things too numerous to mention. Some people were respectful and gracious about any help they received, but others were not.

At one point, I was the only person working in the church on Fridays and I came to dread the day. It was a big church with nine or ten outside doors and most of the time I was not allowed to lock them. Needless to say, it made me uneasy to know that anyone could walk in off the street and hide somewhere in the building or just come directly to my office and do me harm. And we had some scary looking people walk through those doors. Things were often stolen from the church by some of those people. There was no way I could watch the whole church, even if I hadn't had work to do in my office. Someone stole our TV equipment that was used to broadcast our morning services. Thankfully, when it was discovered and an insurance claim filed, the new equipment which cost about the same as the old was much better and more updated. That was a pleasant surprise.

Someone broke into the church and stole candy from the pastor's office one night, and as I learned later, took money from my desk drawer that had come from some church t-shirts I had sold, and they also stole some of the t-shirts that were still in my office. We could tell that the door had been jimmied open but thought at first that nothing had been bothered. The thief even sold the t-shirts he found to a member of our church who bought them to resell, not knowing they were stolen.

Another time, someone came in through a window they had pried open in the day care director's office and took a ring of keys she had hanging inside the door to the lobby. A year or two later when the IGA across the street was having work done on something on the roof of the store, they found that ring of keys. When the culprit was caught, he admitted throwing the keys up on the roof after breaking into the church and stealing the things mentioned above, as well as some things from the kitchen. Thankfully, after installing a security system, there were no more break-ins while I was there.

Some of the people who came in frightened me, as I was concerned about their sanity. One was a strange man with adhesive tape on his glasses who came in, handed me a phone number and said it was for some bus company and that you could call that number and get a schedule for anywhere the bus line went. He seemed to think he was doing me a great favor that I would be eager to repay. I've never taken a bus in my life except for a trip to Fort Smith when Heavener had bus service back when I was a kid. And I wouldn't know where to go now if I wanted to catch a bus.

Then he asked me to buy him some new glasses. And he became very irate when I told him I had no way to do so.

At one point we had a course on "spiritual gifts" and one of mine was "discernment." I didn't understand it too well till I started thinking back through the years and realized that most of the time, my very first impression of someone turned out to be very close to the way they actually functioned. I don't like to think of that as being judgmental. Usually I had nothing to base that feeling on except a gut feeling I got the first time I met them. But that "gift" came in handy working in the church office.

Usually someone could walk in the door and I could almost tell you their story before they opened their mouth. Not to say that some were not on the level, but so many were just taking advantage of every church they could. What they said as a rule didn't mean much, because so many of those people had a line they used so often they could almost sing it. But once in a while I got a real surprise.

I've never had a problem with helping people who are really in need, and especially if it's through no fault of their own. But through the years I've seen, and been the victim of, so many scams that it's hard not to get cynical.

For example, many years before I started that job, we were attending a small country church. There was a needy family in the community that our church helped through some tough times. The man had a drinking problem and the woman had to undergo a rather serious surgery. There were four boys at home. Our church took food to the family, we women cleaned the house with the woman's blessing, and we helped in any way we could.

Several years later, the man and woman were divorced and she and the boys were living down the street from us. By this time we had moved our membership to a church in town, the one where I would later work. One day an announcement was made in church that a family was in need of help. Their house had burned and they had lost everything. There were four boys who needed clothes for school, and they would also like to attend our church if they had the needed clothes. We had no idea who the family was, but we gave to the cause.

Later a woman in our church called and asked me if I could give her any more information on the family, mainly pertaining to family income. When I told her I didn't know who the family was, she said they lived just down the street from us, and she told us their name.

It really irritated me because I knew that family had moved out of the house that had burned two weeks before the fire. In fact, in passing their current place of residence only a few days prior, I had seen clothes on the clothesline that I recognized as the woman's from having seen her wear them before the fire. The youngest of the four boys was in our son's class in school, and he often came to the house to visit Jim. That was during the time that white jeans were in style, and Jim had a pair of them that he had outgrown. Steven was smaller than Jim, so we passed them on down to Steven. From then on, Jim often came home with requests from Steven's mother, through Steven. She would like to have a pair of white jeans for each of the other three boys. Steven needed some new socks for school. I felt sure that she was drawing a welfare check on those boys and just mooching off anyone she could. I wouldn't have minded to help them, even if we really had little to spare at the time, but I just felt that she was using anyone she could. After that, Steven sometimes came to our church, but if any of the others in his family ever did, even after the church was so good to help them, I never knew of it.

So when I took the church job, I was prepared. But not well

enough. As ours was the only church in town with a full-time secretary, and it was located a block from the main highway and from the railroad on which transients often "borrowed" a ride, we were the prime target in town for anyone in need of help.

I had no problem with the requests for food, and wrote many food vouchers for the needy to take to the store across the street and buy food. But I heard so many outlandish stories that I came to distrust most of them.

Our new and younger pastor learned that many people were hitting five or six churches a day, and it was never known till the treasurer of the Ministerial Alliance went to pay the bills for the vouchers given by those churches. It was our pastor's suggestion that the churches rotate month-by-month to give out vouchers, so if people came to one church requesting help and it wasn't their month, they could be referred to another church. That way they couldn't hit numerous churches in a day's time.

He also instituted the policy of asking anyone who requested help to do an hour or two of work at the church, under the supervision of the custodian. They were never to be asked to do anything strenuous or dangerous. Maybe wash a window or two or some other small job. The idea, I suppose, was to give a sense of dignity to anyone asking for help. It was also a good way to get a feel of the situation with one asking for help. One day a man came in and told me had been hitchhiking for days, all the way from Tennessee, he was having trouble with hemorrhoids, and needed a tube of cream for the problem. I called the local store for a price for the product, and was prepared to write him a voucher for it. Then I called in the custodian and explained to the man the policy regarding working for help. The custodian asked him about doing some minor job, to which he replied, "I'll be happy to do it, but first let me go move my car closer to the church." When asked where it was, he replied that it was two or three blocks away.

As he walked out the door, I told the custodian, "He won't be back." When asked why, I replied that he had said he had been hitchhiking for days. So one way or the other, he was lying. And he had no intention of doing any work. We felt that he had wanted money for alcohol or drugs and had made up the story about his hemorrhoids. He never returned.

Another man came in asking for gas to take his live-in girlfriend to the doctor. I told him he would be required to work for an hour to earn the money. He said it was almost time for her appointment, so could he come back that afternoon and do the work? I agreed to it, knowing he wouldn't return till he needed more money. When I went by the store to pick up some groceries on my way home from work, one of the checkers told me about the man coming in to redeem the gas voucher. He had said, "Do you know what they wanted me to do for this? They expected me to work for them for an hour!" She had told him that she had to work for everything she got, as did most other people. Needless to say, this man was put on the "do not help" list.

Another local woman hit the churches every month requesting help for food. The first time she came in after I went to work there, she told a pitiful story about having cancer and all the bad news that goes with that. After that she was there every month. After the changes were made where the churches rotated months to give help, she came by every month to ask me which church was responsible for "helping" that month. One of our members saw her in Wal-Mart on the first of the month with two carts full of things that wouldn't be considered needful at all. At that time her name went on the "do not help" list.

When word was passed around that our church would be

giving out Thanksgiving baskets and people needed to sign up at the church, a woman whose voice I recognized from years before called and told a sad story about a woman who needed to be put on the list. I recognized the name of the person as her daughter. Later the daughter called, not knowing she was talking to someone she knew, and had her mother's name put on the list. That was common practice with a number of local people.

One woman came in off the street and asked if the church would pay for her prescription for an inhaler. She wouldn't get paid "till Friday" (a statement I heard often) and she really needed her medication. I asked her how much it cost and proceeded to call the treasurer of the Ministerial Alliance and the drug store to see if we could do it. Meanwhile, she stood across the office from me, hanging onto the door frame, wheezing and coughing till I fully expected her to drop dead before my eyes.

When I finished making my phone calls, I held out the voucher and as she crossed the room to take it, I told her the price had apparently gone up on the prescription. As she reached for the voucher and exhaled, the overpowering smell of cigarette smoke almost knocked me down. She said, "I'm not surprised it's gone up. It's getting so I can hardly afford to buy cigarettes." It was my last day on that job and I had just had it. I told her that maybe if she quit smoking, she wouldn't need the inhaler. She said, "Well, I have hereditary emphysema, so it wouldn't do any good."

I always dreaded days when I was alone in the church. Sometimes men came in drunk or high on drugs and I found it very unnerving. One day a man came in, not asking for anything except information. He said he was an alcoholic who had been trying to quit drinking, but at Poteau he had "fallen off the wagon." He woke up in his truck with his head in his tool box, and his wallet missing. He was taken to jail and when he was released, found that he had lost all his identification, and the law wouldn't release his truck till he paid his fine. He did have a checkbook in the truck, on a bank in Texas, where he lived, and he swore he had money in the bank there, but nobody would cash a check for him. The law would not take a check, nor would any of the banks at Poteau. So he had walked the fifteen miles to Heavener to check at the banks here, only to hear the same story. No ID, no checks taken.

I called the Texas number listed on his check and let him talk to someone at the bank. They told him they could give him no help over the phone. Then I asked to talk to them. I asked if they could tell me if the man had money in their bank. The lady said she couldn't tell me. I felt that if he were unknown to her or if she knew he had no money there, she would have told me that. So I assumed he was telling the truth.

He went on to say he had a cousin who lived about 50 or 60 miles southeast of our town, and she might help him. He couldn't remember her married name, only that she ran a video store in a certain little Arkansas town. I looked in our national church directory for a church in that area, and after a call or two, located a church secretary in that area who knew the woman. She said the man's cousin had sold the video store and now she and her husband were running a convenience store in the area. She gave me the phone number for the store and I called it and let the man talk. Unfortunately, the couple was out of town for the day.

During all this time, the man told me he had been in prison twice for drug crimes and that if he ever went back to prison it would be for life. He said he had a mental problem and was out of his medication, and that all he wanted was to find someone who would take his check to pay for a room where he could wash out the clothes he was wearing and get a few hours' sleep. Maybe I should have been afraid, but for some reason, I wasn't. I told him that the Ministerial Alliance would pay for a room for the night for him, since the cold temperature outside fell within the range required by the Alliance to pay for a room, but he said he didn't want anyone to pay for it. All he wanted was for someone to let him pay for one with his check. So I called the motel north of town and asked for the price of a room for the night. I told them the man was coming there so please give him a room and the Alliance would take care of it. I also called the treasurer of the Ministerial Alliance and told him what was going on, and that I would drop the man's check made out to the Alliance off with him on my way home. And that I would appreciate a call from him after the check was processed.

Before the man left, I went in the church kitchen and found a box of washing powder and an empty jar under the sink. I filled the jar with washing powder and gave it to him to use for washing his clothes. I also gave him a voucher for $5 to buy some food across the street at the IGA, and suggested he walk downtown to the Mental Health clinic and see if someone there could help him get his prescription filled. He seemed appreciative and relieved with what help I had been able to give him. I told him he could come back to the church the next morning and we'd let him try again to call his cousin, but I never heard from him again. I could only pray that things worked out for him.

The strange thing was that through all of this and in spite of all the things this man had told me about himself, I never felt a moment of fear in spite of the fact that he was there for at least an hour and during all that time not another person came in. There were others who would come in with some sad story and act innocent enough, but I would feel terror in my heart.

A few days later, the treasurer of the Ministerial Alliance called and told me the man's check had gone through with no problems at all.

* * *

At one point, my office had been temporarily moved to the back of the choir room and just inside the east door, into what had formerly been a closet for the choir robes. The building was going through some renovations and my former office was now a part of the bigger plan. Sometimes people had a bit of trouble finding the church office for a while, but the ones you'd perhaps rather not deal with were always the first to find it.

One day I was busy in my closet-sized office when a stranger came barging into the choir room from the outside door. He was bold and brash and pushier than I liked. He appeared to be clean and his clothing was as good as most I saw people wear every day. But he announced that he needed some more clothes. I told him that I was sorry, but I couldn't help him. For the time being, our church had no clothing to give. I didn't bother to explain that our clothing ministry had been put on hold after a lady had fallen into the empty baptistery and suffered a head injury when she had come looking for the clothing room. But that's another story so I won't go into it now. Suffice it to say that we had no clothes to give at that time.

He acted like he didn't believe me. Just the same as called me a liar. But he finally left.

The next morning he was back bright and early, wearing a different set of clothes, and again, he looked clean and as good as most people I saw on a daily basis. He stopped in front of my door, gave a big sigh, and said, "Well, I still don't have any more clothes."

And I replied, "And we still don't have any to give."
Where do these people come from, anyway?

* * *

During the time my office was in the choir room, a strange man came in and stopped at my office door. He told me that he had driven to a city east of here, perhaps Little Rock or maybe Nashville, TN, had been standing beside his luggage talking to a man as he was checking into a hotel there, and had become careless about watching his luggage. It had been stolen. And his money had been in his luggage. Of course I always wonder how that happens. Who keeps their money in a suitcase? I thought that was what wallets/billfolds were for. However, he wasn't asking for anything but permission to park his car under the pecan trees out back of the church and take a nap. He said it was his own fault that he had lost his money, and he didn't have the nerve to call his wife in Texas and tell her what had happened. I told him the restroom was right across the hall, and gave him permission to park his car out back. When I came back from lunch, I saw his car still there and for some reason I noticed that he was running a "donut" on one of the wheels. When he later came in to thank me for letting him park out there, and to use the restroom, I asked him if he was driving on a spare and he said yes, a tire had blown out and the donut was all he had. But he didn't ask for help. I knew a young man who ran a local tire shop, called him, and asked if he might have a used tire that he could mount on the man's rim and what he would charge to do that. He gave me a very reasonable price and I asked him if he would do that for the man and send the bill to the Ministerial Alliance. I learned later that the man had accepted the offer. As he left, I also gave him a $5 voucher for food at the IGA. In the

90's, $5 would buy enough food to feed you a time or two if you were careful about how you spent it. My feeling was that we all do stupid things sometimes and need a hand up, and that we should give our fellow travelers on this old earth a little help when we can.

I loved everyone in our church, but I found that the oldest ladies' class was kinder to me than anyone else while I was serving as secretary. I remember trying to lose weight, a life-long struggle, and at the time was off sweets. That very morning one of those dear old souls brought me in a plate of delicious cookies that she had made for me. They looked out for me! Later, the teacher of that class asked me to start teaching the class and let her take a break. I told her that everyone in that class had forgotten more than I would ever know about the Bible. She received that admission kindly and said, "We'll all help you." And they did. It was a great learning experience for me and I learned to love those dear ladies like the grandmothers I never had.

Buying Fishing Gear

Posted on Facebook in May, 2016

I'm too wound up to go to sleep so thought I'd come to the computer to try to unwind. Not that anyone cares, but I thought someone might be interested in what we got each other for our 57th anniversary. Care to guess? We do tend to be different in most situations and this one is no exception.

For a few months, we've been talking about starting going fishing again. Our son Jim says he enjoys fishing, and we enjoy catching fish. There is a difference, and he's right about it. But we just need to get out and do something from time to time and that's about all we could think of that we're both still able to do. So Clem went through all our old fishing gear from back in the good old days, and found little worth using. Not that we ever had that much, anyway. So after discussing it a bit, we went to Walmart to see about buying some new stuff.

I used to pride myself on putting the worms or minnows on the hook and not having to ask him to do it for me. It didn't bother me that much. But now I find I'm getting soft in my old age, and I don't want to put a hook into a living creature, be it worm or minnow. Should I actually catch a fish, I can see getting it off the hook as a kindness, and I don't think I'd mind that. So he bought me a new cheap rod, the one I wanted, as near like my old one as we could find. I think it cost $12.84, which is probably about what it's worth and probably too much to spend on one for me to break. He wanted to buy me one of those costly open-faced contraptions that I never did learn to use without getting the line hopelessly tangled. But I didn't want it. If I couldn't use one when I was young, I sure wouldn't be able to now. He insisted I hold it in my hand and see how it felt. It almost unjointed my arthritic thumb, so I rejected it again. So he found me the cheaper one I wanted and asked what I thought about the color. It was pink. I didn't want a pink one. I'm not six years old and I don't do much pink anyway. And I hope I still look enough like a female not to need a pink fishing rod to identify my gender. So he found me a red one. It doesn't matter to me what color it is as long as it's not pink.

Then he wanted to know what else I wanted. I said, "Fishing line, a weight, a hook, and a bobber." (Reminded me of one of our granddaughters who, at the age of four, having recently been introduced to fishing, requested for her Christmas present, "A pole, a line, a hook, and a "wum." ")

He asked what lures, etc. I wanted. I saw some dead shad in a package and surmised that I might not mind putting a hook into something that was already dead. But I don't think he bought any of those. Some of the lures cost more than my shoes and I just didn't like the idea of hanging them up in a tree and having to go off and leave them there. So I finally picked out a package of some kind of rubbery things, and then convinced him to pick out anything he needed or wanted and let me go shop for groceries.

He brought home a good assortment of things he deemed useful for fishing. This included a tackle box, the usual weights, hooks, bobbers, and lures, and some kind of collapsible wire thing to put fish in, if we caught any, because he remembered when we used to go fishing, we put anything we caught on a stringer. Several times we pulled up a snake wrapped around our fish on the stringer, and a couple of times a turtle. So this way, if we catch anything worth keeping, maybe we won't have to fight the snakes and turtles in order to keep them.

Now that I've bored myself to sleep, I'll head for bed, where I'll no doubt dream of catching a boat load of fish (although we'll be fishing from the bank). Clem will probably dream of going fishing, not getting a single bite, and falling in the water as well.

10/25/2020 Update: We still haven't found time to use that fishing gear. Hope we can find it if we ever have a nice day when we both feel like getting out of bed.

Buying Some Monsters

My granddaughter, Ashley, was a little mercenary even at a very young age. And she was afraid of monsters. We lived in an old house and had built a large room in the attic. The room had a long, narrow closet between it and the rest of the attic. There was a door that led into the rest of the attic that had not been converted. Ashley was always afraid of that closet and the part of the attic beyond. She just knew there were monsters living in there.

I tried and tried to convince her that we had no monsters in our house. But she would never believe me. So finally I was inspired. I would put it in a language she could understand. I told her, "Ashley, we don't have a single monster in this house. We can't afford any monsters."

She didn't say anything, but appeared to be mulling over the situation. When she got home, she said to her mother, "Mommy, did you know that you have to buy monsters?"

So I'm hoping she's very happy now that she has grown up and married, because she lives in a big house and I'm pretty sure she could afford to buy several monsters if she found any she liked.

Aliens in the park

We should have already been in bed by that time, but as we sometimes tend to do, we had piddled around at this thing and that until it had become quite late--well past our usual bedtime. Right now I don't remember what either of us was doing, but that part is not important. Seems to me I was probably getting ready for bed when my husband appeared with a puzzled look on his face.

"Will you come and look at something and tell me what you think?"

For clarity in this report, I need to explain the layout of the land here. We live on the down side of a road that runs parallel to and just below the top of a hill, and is the western border of the city limits of Heavener. Our neighbor Betty lives next door to us on the south, and between her driveway and ours is a strip of land we refer to as "the park." When Betty and her husband moved next door to us, he had just been diagnosed with cancer, and he lived about two years after they moved here.

One day shortly after moving in next door, she said to me, "Let's make a park between our driveways." The area between our driveway and hers was basically a somewhat unattractive rectangle of scruffy trees, weeds, and grass. This was new construction out here at the time so we hadn't been here too long ourselves. We really didn't care that much what that area looked like anyway, so had done nothing to it short of getting rid of the briars and weeds and picking up fallen tree limbs. Of course only a narrow strip of it was ours and the rest of it was hers. But knowing she needed something to take her mind off her husband's illness, I agreed to work with her to build a park.

The two of us hauled rocks by the pick-up load from an area creek bed, dug two holes in the ground, a large one and one not so large, lined them with rubber sheeting, and built two ponds and waterfalls. We started putting in plants from the nursery here and there and she added various tables, chairs, swings, rocking chairs, hanging baskets, flower-filled antique washing machines, rock walks, a cactus bed---you name it. She loves that park and thrives when she works in it. It overwhelms me. Through the years, I've pretty much backed off and left it to her. My husband mows the small part that belongs to us when he mows the rest of our yard, I try to rake the leaves off our side once or twice a year, and that's pretty much the extent of our involvement with it these days.

Across the road from the park is an empty lot that extends from the road to some undefined line on the other side of the hill. I think the owner of the house to the south end of the lot now owns it, but for a long time it sat empty and neglected. Now it looks a bit park-like itself.

Back to my story. Seems my husband had, for some reason, looked out the kitchen window towards the road and what he had seen had upset him a bit. Now I was looking as well. It appeared to me that there were lights of various colors appearing at the top of the hill across the road and moving down the hill, across the road, and into the park. I went to a window in the south end of the house and looked out. What I saw chilled me to the bone.

Right next to the front of Betty's house one of the lights seemed to have separated itself from the others. It appeared to be moving around, changing from green to red to blue but remaining in the same general area, like a sentry on duty. I fought down the impulse to call and warn her to make a hasty exit out her back door and flee.

In my mind's eye, I could see a spaceship parked just over the top of the hill across the road from the park. Aliens were pouring out of the spaceship, bearing lights of various colors, crossing the road and coming through the park, and would soon be upon us. I must have been in a state of shock, seeing things going on that I had previously experienced only in scary movies.

Let me emphasize here that I'm not a person who tends to panic over imaginary events, or anything else for that matter. I'm usually the level-headed one who can figure out how to handle a crisis. But I also have never had a closed mind.

While I've never been sure if I believed in aliens in space ships or not, I've never called anyone who claimed to have seen one a liar. I've always had a barely conscious fear of being taken into a space ship and having various physical tests run on my body before being returned to the real world. But at the same time, I've never actually thought it would happen. Now I wasn't so sure.

My husband decided he would walk up the driveway to the road and see what he could find out. I thought he had lost his mind. I begged him not to go. Of course, being a man and my protector, he felt he had no choice.

So he walked slowly up the driveway and soon I could see him no more. Pictures of little green men hauling him into their space craft and starting to work on him appeared in my mind. He has a morbid fear of most things medical, at least if it involves being put to sleep, so I was suffering for him.

It seemed to me he had been gone an awfully long time. Finally I crept out the front door, sans porch light, stood on the edge of the porch and called his name. Nothing. The hair stood up on the back of my neck. I rushed back inside and locked the door. Wondering what to do next, I peeked from the kitchen window, hoping to get at least a glimpse of the man I'd been married to for the last 54 years. I was too embarrassed to even pray. I toyed with the idea of calling 911 but feared the repercussions of that. So I just waited.

Finally, after what seemed an eternity, he was at the door and I was opening it. He asked, in the same tone he would use if he had mislaid his eyeglasses, "Did you know Betty had put those new lights up in the park? There are green, red, and blue ones that flash on and off randomly. If you let your imagination go wild, especially from below the park, it looks like they're marching down the hill, crossing the road, and creeping through the park."

Shortly afterwards, having already had my nightmare for the night, I went to bed and slept peacefully.

Cousin Helen and the Hell's Angels

My dad's cousin Helen was 75 years old before I ever met her face-to-face. Daddy had been gone for a number of years and his half-brother in California kept urging me to call Helen, who lived in Oklahoma City at the time. I finally got around to calling her but never met her till I left my purse in a treatment room at McBride Bone and Joint Clinic in Oklahoma City and didn't miss it till we got back to Poteau.

Helen lived just a few blocks from the clinic. I called her to ask her to see about picking up my purse and keeping it for me. As luck would have it, she had an appointment there the next day and was happy to oblige.

When we went to pick up the purse, I found that Helen lived in a small house in a somewhat run-down neighborhood. I was pleased to see that the inside was clean as a whistle and tastefully decorated.

I was also impressed with Helen's snow-white hair, twinkling brown eyes, and youthful outlook.

She said that when her daughter had been in law school in Oklahoma City, she had bought a house to live in while she was there, and Helen had later bought one nearby so she could be near her daughter. Then Terri finished law school and moved away. Helen was pretty well settled by then and knew she couldn't follow Terri every time she moved, so she had stayed on. But by the time we met her, she was wanting out of the neighborhood.

A teen-age hoodlum lived next door with his mother who couldn't control him. He constantly harassed Helen and her gentle white dog that she sometimes tied out front to get some fresh air. One day Helen came home to find the glass front door broken, and knew without asking who had done it.

The next time she saw the boy outside, she called him over and tried to talk some sense into him. She finally realized she was wasting her time and was feeling really desperate. She said, "I don't know where it came from, but suddenly the idea popped into my head to tell him I had a good friend who was a member of the Hell's Angels and that he watched out for me."

She could tell the boy didn't believe her, and she felt foolish and guilty for telling such a story.

Shortly afterwards, a younger friend of Helen's called and said she was going to be passing through OKC and would stop by to see her. Imagine Helen's surprise when a couple dressed all in black leather rode up to her house on a motorcycle. It was Helen's friend and her boyfriend.

Helen told them about her problems with the boy next door and sheepishly confessed the story she had told. As the friends were about to ride away a couple of hours later, the boy came out of his house and started walking down the street. Helen saw the motorcycle swing over to the curb and saw that thc Harlcy driver was talking to her neighbor.

Later her friend relayed the conversation that had taken place. The driver had said, "Hey man! Howya doin'? You takin' good care of my friend Helen?"

The young man assured him that he was.

The rider went on, "I really appreciate that, because I don't take kindly to anyone who bothers her."

Shortly afterwards, the boy's mother sent him to some kind of boy's school or home for delinquent boys, and he was gone for a number of months. Did his mother fear for his safety from the Hell's Angels? I don't suppose anyone will ever know for sure, but when he came home, until the day Helen sold out and moved to South Carolina, he never bothered her again.

Brighten the Corner Where You Are

This morning at Aldi's in Fort Smith, the place was so full of people you couldn't stir them with a stick. I had a rather long list, so right after entering the store, I picked up two boxes that had just been emptied and put them in my cart. The crowded situation got to me in a hurry, so I put just a few items in my cart and headed for the check-out.

As I approached the long lines at the registers, I realized I had one box that I would have no need for. But I soon noticed that the young Oriental lady ahead of me had an overflowing cart and no boxes at all. I asked her if she could use the box, which she accepted gladly, saying she had completely forgotten that one needs to bring their own containers to Aldi's.

About that time I noticed that a young man who was sort of in the line behind me had a box full of loaves of bread and no cart. He looked quite uncomfortable. The young lady behind me, who was wearing scrubs and who I guessed to be a nurse, had only a few items in her hands, but she appeared to be a person in a hurry.

I didn't have to be anywhere anytime soon, so I asked both the young man with the bread and the lady in scrubs if they would like to go ahead of me in line. I was a bit surprised that they both accepted the offer so quickly. She said she had never shopped there at that time of day before, so had had no idea it would be so crowded. And she was on her lunch break from work.

So the Oriental lady with my box, the man with the bread, and the nurse on her lunch hour, checked out quickly. The young man left the store, the nurse turned back to thank me for the third time, and the Oriental lady stopped before leaving the store to invite me to a program at her church tonight. She spoke to me again in the parking lot as she was loading her groceries. She was a happy, bubbly type who made the day brighter for me.

Later I was thinking about the day's shopping experience and a thought came to me. It's so easy to do small things for other people. I remembered the young lady who last year at Aldi's gave me her shopping cart, still bearing the quarter she could have retrieved when parking the cart, wished me a Merry Christmas and rushed off to her car. A quarter wouldn't make or break me, but it did give me a good feeling to know a stranger had noticed a drab old woman and cared enough to do me a favor. I think that's what life is all about: noticing the ones around us and doing any little thing that might brighten their day. You can never know how much difference it might make in their lives.

There was a time when my husband was waiting in the car while I ran into Wal-Mart at Poteau to pick up a couple of things. A man from Heavener who I knew only on sight, came up and started talking to me and couldn't seem to stop. I stood there with him for quite a long time, then remembered that Clem was waiting for me and we still had to go on to Fort Smith. So I told him as kindly as possible that I had enjoyed visiting with him but that I just had to go. That night he killed himself. I don't flatter myself by thinking that he cared one way or another about what I said or did, but it will always haunt me to think that maybe if I had just taken a few more minutes to visit with him, it might have made a difference in his attitude towards himself. If a stranger cares enough to talk to me, maybe my life is worth something after all. We just never know. I hope I never forget that.

Bridge Collapse Disaster near Gore

The Minneapolis bridge collapse a few years ago brought back to Oklahomans the memory of the too-recent bridge disaster over the Arkansas River near Gore, Oklahoma. The main difference here was that one of the main supports on the Oklahoma bridge was struck by a barge. A number of people lost their lives when their vehicles fell into the water. Fortunately, some were saved by fishermen who happened to be in boats near the bridge.

This bridge was one which was much higher in the middle than on either end. The west end of the bridge collapsed, while the rest of it remained basically intact. Vehicles approaching the bridge from the east had no visual indication that the west end of the bridge was gone.

A fisherman below, realizing the predicament, wondered how anyone could warn the westbound traffic in time to put a stop to the carnage. He had flares in his boat, but had no idea if they would even work, as they had been there for a long while. He took a chance and fired a flare in the direction of the westbound lane on top of the bridge. It landed right in front of a tractor-trailer rig which had already driven onto the bridge from the east end. The driver slammed on his brakes, jackknifing the truck, which effectively blocked all west-bound traffic. The fisherman, amazed that the flare had worked, tried firing another one, only to find that it performed as expected—traveling only a few feet before fizzling out. He felt that the first had been guided by divine intervention.

My husband and I had driven over that bridge about a week earlier on our way home from visiting our son in Muskogee. We were planning to pull our fifth-wheel trailer up there soon, and wondered how the crosswinds on the high bridge would affect the stability of the trailer.

On the day of the bridge collapse, we were driving through Arkansas, when, 11:00 a.m., our cell phone rang. It was some younger friends from up the road who knew we often drove on the area of the interstate on which the bridge was located. They had started trying to contact us the minute they heard of the incident and were becoming alarmed that we hadn't answered our home phone. They said they were about ready to drive up to the site of the collapse and look for us.

A few minutes later our son called. He had heard of the collapse while at church, and had rushed out to call us on his cell phone. He, too, was afraid we might have been on the bridge.

Of course we were grateful to have been spared from the accident. But as reports started coming in of missing people and later of the bodies found in the water—one whole young family, an older couple, various individuals—we could almost feel the despair of their families. Had they called and called to check on their loved ones, growing more and more frantic each time the phone rang? How hard it must have been to know their loved ones were in that cold water and they would never see them alive again!

One older couple who perished in the bridge collapse had had their house destroyed by a tornado a few years earlier. They had not been injured in the tornado, and had rebuilt their house. I wondered if they might have felt they had had their share of disasters and could now rest easier. It was one of those things that just proves what we had been talking about earlier. Any time you leave your house, you should do so with the knowledge that you may never be back. We try to always part with any family member or friend with that in mind, and let them know that we love them.

The Trip of a Lifetime

My husband and I had always wanted to travel abroad, but had never found the time, money, opportunity, and courage all at the same time. In April 2008 everything came together at one time, and we finally had the opportunity.

Clem's nephew has taught school on air bases in England and Holland for almost 20 years, and had been on us for years to come over for a visit. For most of those years, one or both of us had a job to consider, and for the last several years I hadn't been physically up to doing all the walking we had been warned would be necessary in order to see many of the sights in England.

Last Spring, Doug called and said if we ever planned to come, we'd better get with it, as he didn't plan to stay in England forever. I had had a hip replacement which had put me back on my feet and given my life back, and I felt up to any challenge. Clem had retired, again, a year earlier, and although he had broken ribs and back problems caused by a fall from a ladder, he decided to try it anyway.

We left Tulsa early on April 2nd, flew to Dallas, and then on to New York, according to the logic of airlines. We arrived in the airport in New York City with hours to spare, and made all the preparations for our overseas flight. An hour prior to our 6:20 p.m. flight time, we bought some sandwiches for supper, Clem bought a Coke, and we were sitting in the departure area, feeling as relaxed as possible under the circumstances. I asked him to pour a little of his Coke into a folding cup I had with me.

Suddenly everything changed. An announcement came over the speakers informing us that our flight had been cancelled. We were to go to luggage carousel 3, claim our luggage, and report to ticketing. At that announcement, my folding cup collapsed and its contents spilled down the front of my light blue shirt. I made a swipe at the mess with a napkin, then we fled to claim our luggage. I can't imagine what the rush was, as the rest of the evening was wait, wait, wait.

I went to the baggage claim area to retrieve our luggage while Clem went to locate the ticketing counter. Once I had dragged all our luggage off the carousel, I stacked it up into two stacks, on top of the two largest suitcases, and rolled it into the restroom, where I retrieved a clean shirt from one of the bags and changed into it. A few minutes later, I saw Clem coming for me.

We took the luggage to a long line in the ticketing area, and proceeded to wait. And wait. And wait. There were numerous English citizens in that line, anxious to get home after being in New York for a few days. One woman was actually in tears, and there were many cross words passed between some of them and some of the agents. Most of them eventually made arrangements to fly into Heathrow Airport in London, but we were hesitant to do so, because we were supposed to fly into Stansted Airport, which is closer to Doug and Kathleen's home, and they were supposed to meet us there.

Even knowing it was the middle of the night in England, I took a chance and dialed Doug and Kathleen's number. We had no idea if our cell phone would even work over there. It did, and Kathleen answered. I asked if we should go ahead and fly into Heathrow or wait for the next flight to Stansted 24 hours later. She said it would be best to wait for the next flight into Stansted.

So here we were, in the airport, in New York City, and nowhere to go for 24 hours. Years earlier when we had driven to New York City and became technically lost in downtown Manhattan, I had promised the Lord I would never go to New York City again if He would just get us out of the place safely. I had let myself out of that promise by saying we wouldn't actually be in New York City—but just in the airport long enough to change planes. So much for my plans.

Once we reached the agent and told him we had decided to wait for the next flight to Stansted, he gave us vouchers to stay in the Ramada Inn, which he said was basically on airport property, a voucher for a taxi ride back the next day, and three food vouchers for $20 each. He then called a taxi, which was supposed to meet us at the door. We dragged all that luggage out the door, and stood waiting at the curb for about an hour, getting colder by the minute. It's COLD in New York in April. We were rushed by a herd of taxi drivers, but none of them was the one we were waiting for. Finally, Clem called the number he had been told to call the next day, and the man who answered claimed to be waiting in a different location. But he did arrive within the next few minutes, loaded up our luggage, and drove us to the hotel.

Once there and checked in, we went to the restaurant area and checked on the availability of food for the following morning. A buffet breakfast would be $13.95 each. We're used to eating toast for breakfast, and decided we just wouldn't be willing to pay the difference between the voucher and what it would cost us to eat food we wouldn't ordinarily eat anyway.

As soon as we could get around the next morning, we caught the hotel's shuttle bus to the airport, rather than risk dealing with another taxi. Once there, we found our vouchers would buy enough food at the airport to serve us well all day. So we took advantage of it.

Our flight finally left late in the afternoon and the flight to England was uneventful, but we never slept a wink on the whole overnight flight. And once we landed, the circus started again.

When the plane had been parked and the "fasten seat belts" lights turned off, we, along with the other passengers, gathered up our carry-ons and lined up to leave the plane. We had advanced half the length of the cabin when the line stopped. We put down our carry-ons to wait. Then the pilot announced he was going to have to move the plane a bit, so we needed to get back in our seats.

Once we were off the plane and headed for luggage and customs, we were rushing down a hallway when we saw restrooms. I said I should probably stop, but felt sure there would be more near the luggage carousels. So we went on down the hall and down an escalator at the end of the hall.

At the bottom of the escalator, Clem suddenly made a grab for his side and exclaimed, "I've left the camera on the plane!" He had set the bag down when we were waiting in line to leave the plane before we were sent back to our seats. And he had failed to pick it back up. We looked around for an up escalator, stairs, anything, and there was nowhere to go but to continue on the way we were going.

At this point Clem was inspired. So the escalator was going down. So what? He dropped his carry-ons and made a mad dash to run UP the down escalator. Now this was a man a week short of his 70th birthday, with broken ribs, back problems, no sleep for over 24 hours, and exhausted physically and mentally. But he didn't let that even slow him down. As he rushed up the escalator, people coming down were yelling at him, "This escalator is going down!" Wonder if they thought he hadn't noticed that? Amazingly, he made it to the top unscathed and jumped off.

I waited for several minutes before he came back and announced that the doors had locked behind us and there was no way to get back to the plane. So we went on to what we expected to be the luggage carousels. Rounding the corner, we were surprised to see that what awaited us was the entrance to an underground train that would carry us to the terminal. There were no restrooms there. We had thought we were already in the terminal.

I saw a phone on the wall and suggested we might find help that way, so he picked it up and was talking to an airport employee when we saw our crew from the plane coming. He handed me the phone and rushed to meet them. One of the flight attendants who had been visiting with us as the plane was landing told him how to get back to the area near the plane, and instructed him to go there and wait for someone to open the door.

While he was gone, I waited, less and less patiently, for at least 30 minutes, watching the doors to the train open and close every two minutes. By the time he finally returned, having been blessed by helpful people who returned his camera case, containing the camera and two GPS units, I was getting desperate.

We quickly boarded the train, and felt the worst was over. It wasn't. It was probably a two-minute trip to the terminal, but our train stopped just short of the terminal and sat there for at least 20 minutes. There was no way to open the door. We were trapped. An automated voice kept repeating, "We apologize for any inconvenience."

Inconvenience? "Inconvenience" does not even begin to cover the situation when a restroom is the object of your desires, and when a relative is circling the terminal wondering what has become of you.

We were just yards from the airport terminal at Stansted Airport. After sitting there for about 20 minutes, with the air growing more and more stuffy, we were all beginning to lose our patience. I was at the point where if I didn't get out of there soon, I was in danger of losing more than my patience. And I had a feeling I wasn't alone in that.

Finally, a young man came from somewhere in the back and opened the door of a call box on the wall near my seat. He punched some buttons and if memory serves me right, he spoke into the box. I asked him if he had been in this situation before. He said, "No, this is the first time I've ever been here." I don't know who he was, but he seemed to attract some attention, as two men soon came from the tunnel behind us, pried open the door, and led us to an emergency exit behind the train.

This had started out as an underground train but in the couple of minutes we had ridden on it, it had become an elevated train. Go figure.

We went down steps to a grassy area on the level below the train platform. We could have walked to the terminal in a couple of minutes if we had been allowed to do so. But no, we had to wait for whatever it was we were waiting for.

As we stood with our rescuers on a wide concrete walk beside the grassy area, waiting for who-knew-what, a small pickup with "airport security" painted on the door roared up and a short, round man with a red face, wearing a fluorescent green vest popped out. If we were expecting an apology or some expression of sympathy for our "inconvenience," we were to be disappointed.

The man, whose appearance and actions brought to my mind the term, "cock of the walk," came strutting over to our group and shouted, "I WANT TO KNOW WHICH ONE OF YOU HAS BEEN SMOKING IN MY TRAIN!"

For the first time I noticed that several young men who had been in our train car were smoking. I would usually notice it right away, but for once I hadn't. If any of them had been smoking on the train, I had been unaware of it. While there may have been "no smoking" signs on the train, we had seen none after being released from it.

One young man standing just in front of me slipped his cigarette down the side of his leg, dropped it onto the ground, and slid his foot over it. After an awkward pause that must not have been as long as it seemed, another young man stepped up to the "security guard" and said, "I have. So are you going to arrest me?"

Caught off guard, the cocky little guy just stuttered, turned around, and walked back to his truck.

In a few minutes a bus pulled up to the end of the walk and we were instructed to board it. As we were entering the bus, our cell phone rang. Kathleen had been circling the airport, and failing to see us, was about to start efforts to locate us. We were so thankful to find that our cell phone was working on that side of the big pond.

The bus, after a trip of about a hundred feet, pulled up in front of a terminal entrance and we were told to exit and go into the terminal. We could have walked and carried our luggage for that distance in a tenth of the time we had spent waiting for the bus. But no pedestrians were allowed in the area.

Since we had been detained so long before reaching the terminal, we were relieved to see that the crowds had already been through customs and there were no long lines. After a hasty trip to the restroom, we claimed our luggage and went through customs with no problems.

Then, thinking we were home free, we located an outside door in the front of the building, crossed the street, rolling our overloaded bags behind us, and went to the far end of the fence that ran parallel to the street to wait for Kathleen. She had described the area and told us to meet her there. But we soon saw signs proclaiming, "No pick-ups here. Departing passengers only. Violators will face a stiff fine." Two haughty guards in the traditional fluorescent green vests were strutting up and down the walk to discourage anyone with any intention of violating their rules.

One thing that impressed me unfavorably everywhere we went in England was that it seemed you could take anyone in off the street, put a green vest on him and he'd think he was somebody really special.

The last time Kathleen had been at the airport, picking up passengers there was allowed. Rules had been changed without her knowledge. After asking someone for instructions, we dragged our luggage back down the walk, across the street, back through the terminal, down a long ramp, and back out to a spot directly below the place we had been before. Then we called Kathleen to let her know where we were. She said she had been circling the area in front of the terminal, and seeing the new signs, was afraid to stop. She had noticed one of the guards writing down her tag number, but, as she said, there was nothing he could do, since she never stopped.

Finally, after another long walk, we managed to get together. What a relief it was to see a familiar face, a person driving her own vehicle, even if it was on the wrong side of the road.

Kathleen has been driving in England for about 20 years now, so she was comfortable and competent in the surprisingly heavy traffic. Clem and I found the roundabouts especially confusing, which reinforced our conviction that we didn't want to try to drive in England. We made the trip to their house in good time, and what a relief it was to get there!

Before we left home, Kathleen had asked if we/I would like to attend a concert while we were visiting them. She didn't mention that it was in London, because we had said we didn't especially care about going to London; we were more interested in seeing the rural countryside. Clem had no desire to attend a concert, which was good news for Doug, as he didn't want to go either.

Unfortunately, our unplanned overnight stay in New York had made us a day late in arriving in England, and the concert was to be that night. Kathleen had only told me that we would drive for about an hour and then take the Metro (subway/train) for another 45 minutes. I should have known that would mean London, but didn't really care either way.

So, upon arrival at their house, Kathleen said she supposed I would be too tired to go to the concert, considering I hadn't slept in over 24 hours. Surprisingly, I was too wound up to be tired or sleepy, so told her I was raring to go. After a nap of about 45 minutes, I showered and dressed and we were off, leaving Clem and Doug to fend for themselves.

The car trip was interesting but uneventful, as was the subway ride. We caught it at the farthest stop from London, and rode for miles. I was surprised to see very young people riding it alone. At one stop, a father and son got on with their bicycles, splattered with mud, talking to each other about what a great outing they had had that day.

I found the whole set-up very confusing once we were inside London, underground, with trains on both sides of each terminal. Kathleen had a schedule in hand that she read from, but if she had a question, she didn't hesitate to stop any passerby and ask for directions.

We were a little early for the concert, so Kathleen showed me around the area, as much as time permitted. At one museum, there was an empty room almost as large as a football field, with a jagged crack running the entire length of the floor. People were inspecting the crack, and I wondered what had caused it and if people had never seen cracked concrete before. As it turned out, the crack had been "manufactured" for some artistic purpose, and would eventually be filled in.

I enjoyed the concert immensely, as there were a number of guest performers and two guest bands in addition to the main orchestra. The two guest bands were exact opposites, from tie and tails to western dress topped off by matted blond dreadlocks. The more casual-looking group was having such a good time, casting looks among their group that said, "I can't believe we're really performing with the (whatever) orchestra." Their sheer joy was contagious, and I felt especially drawn to them.

After the concert, Kathleen offered to take me to see the Parliament building in all its lighted glory, but it was almost 10:00 p.m., the crowds had thinned out, and I didn't look forward to riding the subway back without the numbers I felt represented safety. I was also getting quite sleepy by then. So we went to the house.

Kathleen had already made travel plans with a friend while we had been trying to decide if we could take the trip to England or not, so she was tied up for the next week. But Doug took his entire week of Spring Break to drive us around to various places in England that we had long wanted to see. Clem was especially happy to get to go to Stonehenge and we visited so many other beautiful and interesting places as well.

Then we took a train to Wales, caught a ferry there, and went to Ireland for a week. After that we returned to England where

Kathleen was back home and she drove us around to many other interesting places while Doug worked at his job.

I'll stop at this point by just saying it was a really great trip—what we both consider the trip of a lifetime, once we actually got there. We wouldn't take anything for the experience. Everything went well until we started home and reached St. Louis, where weather caused our flight to be cancelled. We chose not to take a later flight into Tulsa, as it would have meant getting our daughter or her husband out of bed to meet our plane.

However, our luggage chose to go on to Tulsa, and by the time we finally got there the next day, we found it almost too heavy to load into the car. It apparently had been left out in the rain somewhere, sometime, and everything in the bags was soaked.

But that was a small price to pay for having had such a wonderful trip and making it home unscathed.

Roger Miller and His Arkansas Relatives

Roger Miller was one of my favorite singers. He not only wrote and recorded a lot of silly songs that always lifted my spirits, but in reading about him online, I learned that he wrote many serious songs that were equally good. In fact, his career started off as a writer of songs that were recorded by other artists.

One of my parents' neighbors, Evazee Huddleston, remembered Roger going to school at Cauthron, AR, only a few miles from Heavener. It must have been for a very short time, as from all I can read, he was raised by his uncle Elmer in Erick, a western Oklahoma town. His father died when Roger was a year old, and his young mother couldn't raise the three boys she had been left with. So three of her husband's brothers each took a boy to raise.

Roger's uncle Emmitt ran a store at Cauthron for many years. Maybe Roger had gone to visit for an extended period and enrolled in school while he was there. Whatever the case, Zee remembered his mother coming to get him and take him away to wherever he went after that. She said his mother looked like a very prosperous person, which would have been a shame, considering what a rough time Roger had growing up

We recently learned that Roger was a cousin to my husband's cousin, and had a good relationship with him.

Roger wrote a song, "Billy Bayou" about his cousin Billy Roe Miller, who was Emmitt's son. I had thought that Roger recorded it, and maybe he did later, but Jim Reeves was the first to record it. I didn't see the song as giving a very good description of the Billy Roe I knew, but it is said that at least Billy Roe was the inspiration for it.

My husband's parents are buried in the cemetery behind the property that Emmitt owned. My mother-in-law attended school in the old two-story white schoolhouse that until recently stood across the road from the Methodist church in Cauthron. The road that leads to the cemetery where she is buried turns right beside that old school house, and the Miller place was on that short road.

I was in Emmitt's store several times when we went to Cauthron, before my in-laws passed away. One day Billy Roe was on the phone when we were in the store, and he was telling someone how his mother was the most important person in his life and how no woman could ever come between them. I would have guessed him to be in his late 40's at the time. And I believe his mother had already passed away before then. I knew Emmitt, but never met his wife.

Billy Roe had never married, and if he ever did, I didn't know it. He did bring a woman home with him one time, however, and they lived in the small house behind the store, across the street from Emmitt's big house for a short while.

By this time, Billy Roe was probably in his late 50's, and Emmitt must have been well up in his 80's. Billy Roe and his dad were apparently never close, as he was apparently a mama's boy till his dying day.

The woman Billy Roe was involved with must have learned that Emmitt had some money, and she wanted it. One day she decided she didn't want Emmitt in his own store, and attempted to physically put him out of it. He used his cane to defend himself and she wound up with a broken arm. I think everybody in the community was rooting for poor old Emmitt. I was told that the woman left town and never came back.

Emmitt, of course, eventually died. For some reason I'll never understand, Billy Roe took aluminum paint and painted the headstones on his parents' graves, and on some others as well, possibly his grandparents'. The last time we were at the cemetery, the paint was peeling off, and hopefully in a matter of time will be gone completely.

Not many years ago Billy Roe passed away as well.

I couldn't help comparing him to his successful cousin, Roger Miller. From all the information I can find, Roger spent most of his growing up years on his uncle's farm, doing farm work. He had said that he seldom said anything, and when he did, it was the wrong thing, so he just kept his thoughts inside. He had nothing extra and entertained himself by thinking up the kind of songs that made him famous.

Billy Roe was an only child, born late in his parents' life, and he never wanted for anything. And he never amounted to much.

There must be a moral there somewhere. I guess it's just proof that hard work and deprivation force one to think for himself, and hard knocks are often the making or breaking of a person.

Just a few days ago we were watching a TV show about country music stars through the years. Near the end of the show, they talked about the plane crash that killed Patsy Cline, Hawkshaw

Hawkins, Cowboy Copas, and the pilot, Randy Hughes. After some time had been spent combing the woods where the crash occurred, Roger Miller, who had been involved in the search, drove to a Forest Service tower, climbed it, and spotted the wreckage, which saved much time in the search. Of course that was never mentioned at the time. I just thought it was a proper footnote to Roger's life.

Booker T. Washington—Almost Kin

A number of years ago my husband started punching names into a family tree program for both his family and mine. Somewhere down the line he found a Burroughs who was said to have owned Booker T. Washington. That really got our attention.

A few years later, we took a trip to the Carolinas, Virginia, and Tennessee, where we did some genealogy work. One place we made a point of going was to the Booker T. Washington memorial in Virginia, which was built on the farm of James Burroughs. We arrived there to find a small family cemetery in front of the main park building. In the cemetery, we found the graves of some of the Burroughs family who had owned the farm. They had also owned Booker T., his mother, brother, and sister.

Inside the building, we saw pictures of some of the Burroughs family. The young woman working there said a former employee had done a lot of research on the Burroughs family, and she went to the files and pulled out a folder of information. In it we soon found that the family had a daughter named Ellen America Burroughs. I recognized that name from Clem's information in the family tree program. It was not an easy name to forget.

He went to the car and retrieved a print-out of his research on the Burroughs family and sure enough, there was the entire family, including the same Ellen America. We soon figured out that the owner of the farm and the slaves had been a brother to Clem's great-great grandfather.

That sounds like a long way back, but if my dad were still alive, he would be a great-great grandfather many times over. And his brother whom we visited many times in California would be the same relation to our great-grandkids as this slave owner was to my husband.

My father-in-law was the only older member of the Burroughs family I ever knew, and he was the epitome of goodness and kindness. It was hard to picture relatives of his having owned slaves. Needless to say, neither of us was happy about having slave owners in the family background.

We bought a book written by Booker T. and one written about him and his family. There was some interesting information in those books.

It seems Booker T. was half white and the man who fathered him was reputed to be the "no-account son of a neighbor." Booker T.'s brother, John, also half white, was said to have been fathered by Benjamin Burroughs, who was the obviously "no account" son of John's mother's owner. From Booker's account, John was a wonderful brother and son. In one book I found a picture of John, took it to Clem and asked, "Who does this look like?"

"George," he said. And John did, indeed, bear a strong resemblance to Clem's oldest brother.

One thing that impressed me about John was his willingness to suffer discomfort for his younger brother, Booker. Booker wrote that the only garment he remembered owning till after the slaves were freed was a long shirt made from the leftovers of flax, which he said was so scratchy when new that it was almost unbearable to wear. He said that when his old shirt would wear out and he would have to break in a new one, John would wear it for him long enough to soften it up.

Booker's mother apparently was a Godly woman, but of course she had had no say in who took advantage of her. She was married, but her husband had been sold and transported to another state. His last name was Washington, so Booker T. took that name for his own.

After being freed from slavery and traveling to where their step-father lived, both boys worked at numerous jobs till Booker was finally able to attend college. Although Booker worked all through college, John would send him every penny he could spare to help him out. After Booker T. finished school and became the director of Tuskegee Institute, he sent for John and a boy his mother had adopted, put them through school, and later gave them good jobs.

As for the Burroughs family, Booker wrote that although the "master" was not as hard on his slaves as some were, he apparently still whipped them when they displeased him.

One of the Burroughs daughters took exception to that statement when she read the book years later, saying that her father was "no harder on them than he was on his own children." Booker commented that the youngest Burroughs son, Billy, used to plead for leniency for the slaves when his father was set on punishing them. When Billy was killed in the Civil War, the slaves mourned for him as much as the family did. Billy is buried in the family cemetery in front of the memorial building.

We learned a lot about the Burroughs family on this trip. Most of them were apparently good people, including a medical doctor and a business owner who lived in McMinnville, TN.

But what impressed me most was that someone who started out with absolutely nothing but the shirt on his back, and a scratchy one at that, could become such a wonderful example for the world to follow. Booker T. Washington must have possessed an incredible amount of integrity, wisdom, and a hunger for knowledge.

Today so many people whine about their lack of opportunity in life, using that as an excuse for never amounting to anything. They should read Booker's *Up From Slavery.*

He's the perfect example for anyone who wants to make a difference in the world.

Carla and My Hot Pink Coat

This morning I was cooking oatmeal for us for breakfast and it made me think of a story in a book I read a while back. A young lady had gone to Canada to teach school in a poverty-stricken area where there was basically nothing but a mill, and it was about to have to shut down. There were a number of fatherless kids in that school, due to a horrible accident that had taken a number of lives. Their mothers were just barely able to make it due to a monthly stipend from the mill, and that would soon end. The teacher soon realized that some of the kids came to school too hungry to learn. She talked it over with the few friends she had made in the small town, and they decided they must find a way to feed those kids breakfast because they couldn't learn well on an empty stomach. The only problem was that the teacher and her friends had no money either so they were hard pressed to know how to feed those kids. They finally decided that oatmeal would be the way to go. It was cheap and would fill their stomachs. So they did, after working very hard to get the mothers' permission to feed them without hurting the mothers' pride. And it made a huge difference in the kids' ability to learn.

Thinking about that took me back to my own childhood. We were never rich by anyone's description, but we always had plenty to eat. A new girl in my class lived in a shack on Red Ward's place up on the hill east of Heavener, about three blocks past our house, and she got in the habit of coming by our house to walk on to school with me. Probably the first time she came by, she spotted the leftover breakfast food on our kitchen table. Her eyes nearly bugged out of her head. She said, "Is that real cow's butter? I love cow's butter." Mother, of course, asked her if she had had breakfast and she said no, so naturally Mother told her to sit down and got her a clean plate. I can still see her wolfing down the leftover biscuits and gravy and whatever else there was left. It brings tears to my eyes just thinking about it. I wondered what they did on weekends.

One thing I remember is that there was a beautiful hot pink coat hanging in a closet in our house, waiting for me to grow into it. My sister had already worn it till it was too short for her and now I was eagerly awaiting my turn. And I thought this might be the year. My cousin had sent that coat along with some other things from New York City, where she lived. I have no idea where she got the coat and the other things, but as I recall that was the only time she ever sent us a "care basket."

So on a cool morning Carla came by, wearing something that my mother deemed unfit for cold weather. So she went to the closet and brought out MY COAT. And put in on CARLA! I'd like to say I had another coat that was good enough, but I actually have no idea of what I had for a coat. I do remember at one time a girl down the street who was a little bigger than I was gave me one of her coats that she had outgrown. I wonder now if it could have been that same year. And if her mother might have taken pity on me as Mother did on Carla. It was a very nice coat, far more expensive than anything we would have ever bought, and I appreciated it. But it was so heavy it almost broke my back to wear it. And it was not hot pink.

A few days later Carla told me that she had a gift for our family. It was for the whole family and she was sure we would like it. In my mind's eye I saw a fabulous gift, valuable beyond my wildest imagination. She had been only pretending to be poor to see what we would do, and now that we had given her something special, she was going to return the favor. I could hardly wait till she brought it over on Saturday. I was stunned when I saw the gift. It was apparently very valuable to her and I was touched that she wanted to give it to us. It was a very old, empty compact that Maybelline mascara had come in. It had a tiny mirror in it, which may have been the only mirror they owned. I hope I was gracious about it. I believe it was a great sacrifice for her to make. I had never had much, but I just couldn't wrap my mind around the extent of their poverty.

I don't think I ever got completely over the fact that Mother had given that beautiful coat, the one I had dreamed of wearing for a couple of years, to the little stranger who lived up on the hill and loved "cow's butter." I have to admit that the sting is still there a little when I allow myself to think about it. But I was thankful that I was able to hold my tongue that time and not say anything. I know God uses situations like that to turn lives around and make a big difference in their future. I hope it's in the place where Carla keeps her good memories. If she's even still living.

Carla's family moved away not long after that. I've often wondered whatever became of her but have never heard a word. I guess the one thing she taught me was that while we didn't have a lot, we were rich compared to some people. I hope she has had a good life and has been happy. And that she and the Lord are on very good terms.

St. Barts/St. Barthelemy

St. Barthelemy is a tiny, eight-square-mile island in the Caribbean, about a ten-minute flight from St. Martin. It is surrounded by beautiful, crystal-clear water and white-sand beaches. Shell beach is one exception. The entire beach and for some distance out into the water there is nothing but shells. Clem always wondered why our luggage seemed so much heavier on the return trip. I brought home enough shells to last for a lifetime.

We first saw St. Barts when we took a day trip from St. Martin to St. Barts a number of years ago. For Clem it was love at first sight.

It can be accessed only by boat and small short take-off / short-landing airplanes. The airport starts at the foot of a steep hill and ends shortly thereafter in the ocean. It takes skill to land a plane or to take off from there.

We sometimes stood on the beach at the end of the runway and watched a plane circle the airport for some time before the pilot finally worked up the nerve to try to land it. When he finally succeeded, hoots of approval and applause could be heard all around the airport.

St. Barts is extremely expensive. We were able to spend time there only by employing our usual penny-pinching methods of travel. We stayed in the cheapest motel on the island, which was right on the beach near the end of the runway, and which had the most spartan of kitchen facilities. Eating there was expensive anyway, but we always make a habit of shopping where the locals do, and therefore getting the best prices on food.

There was a small restaurant right on the beach, and we saw signs posted there advertising cheeseburgers for $12.50. It was probably one of the more economical places to eat on the island, but we wouldn't know because we never went near any of the others. I'm thinking by this time the price on cheeseburgers may have doubled. But that's no concern of ours because we won't be buying any of them.

While food was expensive in the grocery stores, by being careful and not wasting anything, we were able to eat about as cheaply as we do at home. While it may not be the gourmet food many people look forward to, it was good enough for us.

St. Barts has a wet side and a dry side. We always stay on the wet side because it's much greener and more attractive.

There's no way to describe the beauty of the place. While the other islands we had seen tended to be somewhat cluttered, with some shacks and shanties, and evidence of poverty all around, Barts wears its pride on its sleeve. The whole island was spic and span. There are many tiny houses, and some of them are undoubtedly old, but we saw none that weren't kept up. Many of them were "hurricane houses" that looked incredibly small for anybody to try to live in. But without exception they were painted white and most had flower boxes under the windows and flowers in the yards.

The hurricane houses have concrete walls which I would estimate to be about 18 inches thick. One of them would be an ideal place to ride out a hurricane. There are also many more expensive houses clinging to the hillsides, with expansive ocean views.

If we were rich, that is where Clem would want to retire. But people in our economic slot couldn't even consider it.

I'm not sure whether or not things are still the same there, as it has been a number of years since we were last there. But the last we knew, the island was owned by or at least supported by France. There were few jobs available on the island, and no taxes. Most who live there were either born there or were wealthy. Clem has checked on real estate prices, and found that if we sold everything we own, we still couldn't afford to buy a postage-stamp-size piece of land with a house the size of our storage building on it. We can't live there, but we can still dream.

Barts is unique in the area in that most of its residents are Caucasian. The prevailing language is French, but enough English is spoken in stores for Americans to get by.

The second time we visited Barts, we learned that there are some women in a small settlement not far from the airport, who make beautiful baskets from the fronds of the Latina palms. When we drove into the area and parked the car, we were soon surrounded by barefoot old women in cotton dresses and bonnets, waving their baskets and babbling something in French. While we couldn't understand their language, we knew they were there to sell us something.

One poor old woman kept pointing to her baskets and saying, "Mahchin! Mahchin!" Her vision apparently had become so dim that she was having trouble seeing well enough to stitch the baskets by hand, so she had resorted to using a sewing machine. I wanted handmade baskets, so told her, "Yes, very nice!" and bought from another woman whose work looked especially good.

This woman's face showed an expression of pride, almost of

taunting, while the old lady with the machine-made baskets looked hurt and depressed. I couldn't get her face off my mind even after we left Barts. I thought of my mother who had once made beautiful, colorful quilts. As her vision dimmed and she sank into dementia, her quilts were often made of clashing colors that reflected her own condition.

We left the area and drove our small rented car back over the 12-foot-wide roads to the motel. Somehow, because of the hurt look on the little old lady's face, I never really liked those baskets, although they are unique.

A year or two later I was still seeing the old lady's hurt look every time I saw those baskets. Finally I told Clem I would like to go back to Barts and buy some baskets from that old lady if she were still living and we could find her. While it might sound like a strange request to anybody else, I knew Clem would jump at any excuse to go back to Barts.

The first thing we did after getting settled into the Tom Beach was to drive back to the area and look for the old woman. I was pleasantly surprised when the scenario was repeated exactly from the time before. The old lady toddled over, showing her baskets and saying, "Machin! Machin!"

I gushed over her baskets and made a big deal of buying something from her. As we drove away I saw a look of triumph on her face, while the one I had bought from before stood there looking confused. Ah! That moment was worth the cost of the trip to me.

While we were on Barts that time, we learned that the Tom Beach had been sold, and soon a multi-million dollar establishment would take its place. We were not happy about it.

When we went to the airport to return home, Clem left me standing in front of the one small ticket counter, surrounded by all the luggage we had brought along, while he turned in the rental car.

The one clerk looked rather bored, and a massive woman in a loud tent dress sprawled in a large chair nearby. I could feel her eyes on me as she said sarcastically, "My, so much luggage! You certainly came prepared, didn't you?"

I grunted some answer to her rudeness and she continued, "Where did you stay on the island?"

"The Tom Beach."

"Oh, you know it's been sold and they're going to tear it down and build a large hotel."

"Yes, we heard."

Then she launched into a litany of complaints about life on St. Barts. Apparently she owned places both there and in New York, and was in the habit of staying on Barts till she became bored out of her mind, then returned to New York. She went on to inform me that we should be staying at a certain hotel that I knew was one of the more expensive ones. She probably owned stock in it.

I had had enough. "We can't afford to stay in places like that. We're just common working people."

The look on her face was priceless. She apparently hadn't expected me to admit what to her must have been obvious. She didn't say another word.

The clerk, though, perked up and suddenly couldn't do enough for me. I could imagine that he had often been forced to listen to the loud woman harassing other travelers and was glad to see her quiet for once. I wondered how long it would last.

Clem dreams of being able to make at least one more trip to Barts in our lifetime. It's highly unlikely that that would happen. But one never knows…

Mumps for All

A few months before our daughter started to school, Clem started to get nervous about her catching the mumps and bringing them home to him. As far as he knew, he had never had them. He had heard that if you catch the mumps before you have children, you may never be able to have any. Thankfully, he was past that point, as we had Sandy and her little brother, Jim, who would have been about a year old at the time.

So one day Clem got up with a sore throat and a lump below his ear. He pulled out the old Medical Encyclopedia and read up on it, and concluded that he had the mumps. We were using a doctor at Mena at the time, but he was out for the day so we had to see another one. I went in the front door and told them what was going on, and they had me tell Clem to go to the back door so he didn't have to go around any of the other patients. The doctor checked him over, confirmed what we already believed, and told him to go home and go to bed. And he added, "And till you get there, walk EEASY."

So he went home and went to bed and had no complications.

However, within a few days' time, both the kids had caught the mumps from him.

Locked Out Again!

I was in the middle of a really busy day in the cake shop when I suddenly realized it was time to pick up my son from school. I put things down, dashed out the door of the cake shop and in the back door of the house, grabbing a ring of keys from a hook by the kitchen door as I went in. I went straight on through to the front door, locked it, pulled it shut behind me, and made a run for the garage. I jumped in the car and reached for the car key. There was none on the ring I had picked up in my mad dash because I had grabbed the wrong set of keys. Unfortunately, there was also not a key to the house in that set.

Since that was before cell phone days, I couldn't call for help even if I had known anyone to call. So I tried to figure out a way to get in the house. I knew the window upstairs over the front porch was unlocked, but it did have a screen over it. That would be the problem. I checked the shop behind the garage, found it unlocked and took a stepladder from there to the front of the house. With some difficulty I was able to climb the ladder and get on the porch roof. I had never realized how hard it would be to get a window screen off without tearing it completely up. And all I had up there to use to try to get it off was one of the keys on the ring I had in my pocket. So in desperation, I tried to pry the screen off with the key. The screen didn't come off, but it wasn't from lack of effort on my part. The key broke off.

I thought about calling my younger brother to come and bring me a key that I always left with my parents for just such an emergency. I would call him. I gave up on the idea of getting in the house without doing major damage to a window or door, and ran across the street to the neighbor's house. Mrs. Williams didn't answer when I knocked on the door, but the wood front door was standing open. I knew where her phone was, and had the insane thought of going on in the house and using her phone anyway. I knew she wouldn't mind, but I really hated to think of going in with her gone. But I was spared from making that decision because the screen door was locked. I knew it because I tried it.

So with no other choice, I started walking towards my parents' house, which was six or seven blocks away. Not a big deal or a long walk for a healthy person. But after walking about a block, I realized I had left home wearing the wrong shoes. I could feel a blister forming on my heel and I really didn't need to get crippled up now with all those cakes waiting to be baked.

So I stopped at a house where I knew the occupants. Not strangers at all, but not close friends, either. I would knock on their door and ask to use their phone. I knocked on the door frame, because the wooden door was standing open. The lady of the house called to me to come in, so I hesitantly opened the screen and stepped inside. Right away I was greeted by a small dog. A mother dog. With young pups. I would normally say a yapping dog, but she was way past yapping. I asked to use the lady's phone and she said it was beside her on a table, and I should come on across the room and help myself. When I started across the room, the dog met me halfway. And bit me. The scary part was that I didn't even care. Somehow it just wouldn't have seemed right if she hadn't bitten me. I used the phone and went out front to wait for my brother. On a day like that when everything else was crazy, why would I have minded being bitten by a small dog?

Bringing Back the Wild Things

When I was in elementary school I read a few stories about how somebody many, many years before had been frightened, chased, or devoured by a bear, wolf, or panther. I would always think how glad I was that none of those ferocious animals were around today, at least in my part of the world.

Even my parents had never come in contact with such animals. The animals had moved on, or out, and now were seen only in the wilds of Alaska or some remote part of distant states.

Somewhere down the line, some bright person decided that the balance of nature had been upset by the eradication of such animals. They got the ball rolling and before long naturalists were reintroducing these animals into civilization. Now we have bears all around us. They have been seen on Poteau Mountain, Rich Mountain, even at Petros. It hasn't been long since one was seen behind our next-door neighbor's house and bear scat behind another neighbor's house. And we live inside the city limits.

We weren't surprised to see them in Yellowstone. They've always been protected in such places. But who ever expected to have to look out for bears anywhere around here, regardless of how deep into the mountains you might venture?

As for wolves, I understand they don't live near us anymore, but at night we often hear coyotes howling. We've even seen several of them at a time in our back yard. Some people don't know the difference between wolves and coyotes. I never thought coyotes were dangerous, but have heard in recent months of cases where they attack people. In fact, one tried to attack our pastor not long ago. They'll also take a pet every chance they get. I've even heard of them attacking small children.

Gilly Robinson said a few years back that a coyote came into his yard and carried off one of his chickens in broad daylight. He rushed in and got a shotgun which he fired at the coyote. He must have come close to hitting it, because the chicken escaped from it and came flying home. I wish coyotes would go the way of the wolves.

A few years ago, we took our three youngest granddaughters to the "zoo" at Queen Wilhelmina State Park. Most of the animals there had been injured and brought to the place to stay until they were well enough to return to the wild. There was a cougar in there, and I was surprised to be told that they were quite common in the mountains around here. Not too long ago, my cousin who lived inside the city limits of Murfreesboro, AR, was up very early in the morning and saw a cougar just outside her yard fence.

I've always known there were a few bobcats around, but had no idea they lived on Timber Ridge Road. In recent years, we have seen several of them in our yard and most of the neighbors have seen them. We often see deer and other small animals, including an occasional fox.

There was a huge old rattlesnake down there at Wilhelmina, and when I tried to look at him, he rattled and hissed at me. It made my blood run cold. There was a sign that said, "It is illegal to kill a snake in Arkansas."

I asked a worker about it and she gave me a long spiel about how long it takes a snake to grow that big, how many pack rats it will eat in a year, etc. She said that if you even run over one on the highway and the authorities can get a copy of your tire tracks, they will track you down and arrest you. For killing a snake? Please.

I don't like rats, either, but if I had to choose between a rat and a snake for a neighbor, the rat would win hands down.

I told her that if a snake trespassed on my property it was asking for it. And of course she said, "Well, there are allowances for special circumstances." Yeah, the circumstances being that I can get my hands on a hoe before it gets away.

Some time back, my neighbor, Betty, and I were out in her pasture looking at rocks we needed to use in a project. Up on top of the pile of rocks, she found strange droppings. I asked her what they looked like and she said, "Giraffe." Just goes to prove my point. I guess now they're bringing them back, too.

The thing I don't understand is why, when it was safe to go out in the wilds and not worry about wild animals, they couldn't leave well enough alone. When it reaches the point where a cougar will attack an adult, carry off a child, or steal a cocker spaniel from somebody's porch, I think it's time to declare war on them. I know I'll have some animal lovers on my case, but think about it. Would you rather protect a cougar or your child?

Some say people have taken over the animals' territory. That may be true. But people have to live somewhere, and after all, animals were put on earth for man's use. If they'll just stay out of my way and leave me and mine alone, I'll be happy to do the same for them.

The Howe Tornado

May 5, 1961 was a muggy day and we were under a tornado watch, as Oklahoma is on many days throughout the spring and fall months. In fact, we can never be sure on any given day throughout the year that a tornado won't come calling.

Late in the afternoon, a number of us were gathered around Short and Evazee Huddleston's storm cellar, watching the sky to the northwest. Suddenly there were exclamations from the crowd as a black, swirling mass of clouds sprang up in the direction of the little town of Howe, which is about five miles north of Heavener.

Some of the older people with more weather knowledge declared it was a tornado. Someone with a transistor radio (a new invention back then) was listening to the local station which is in Poteau, about 12 miles north of Heavener. Within a few minutes, the announcer excitedly conveyed the news that Howe had just been hit by a tornado.

Clem is a native of Howe, and he still had an uncle living there. He wanted to rush up there to check on him, but realized he was very low on gas in the car (a mistake we seldom make since then). That wouldn't have been a problem, except by then the power was off in Heavener as well as Howe, and probably all over the area. We were appalled to realize that gas pumps won't work without electricity. So he just had to sit it out and wonder about the welfare of his relatives till the electricity was restored.

The next day the power was back on and Clem hurried to fill the gas tank so he could go see about his uncle. By then the radio station was constantly updating its list of storm victims, most of whom Clem knew well.

He wouldn't let me go with him to check on his uncle and his family, as I was expecting our first child in about four months and he didn't think it would be good for me to see the aftermath of the storm. So he went alone, and was surprised to be allowed to drive right into the town.

He returned with the news that half the town was almost wiped out. The house on the property where he had grown up had been rebuilt after a fire had destroyed the original house shortly after Clem and his parents had moved out. That house had been destroyed by the tornado, and a young man and his baby were killed when the house was hit. (Strangely, the house that was built to replace the one the tornado took is now standing as a burned-out shell.)

Clem's uncle lived a few blocks from where that house had been. He, his wife, and a teenage daughter had just started to eat their evening meal when they heard the noise of the approaching tornado. Since they didn't have a storm shelter, they ran a block to a neighbor's cellar, and were fortunately unharmed.

Their house was not as fortunate. They returned to find the house still basically in one piece, but the tornado had picked it up, moved it over several feet, and set it down on their dog. His uncle had to cut a hole in the floor to free the dog, which was still alive, but died soon afterwards.

There had been a bowl of strawberries on the table when they left. Although their house was damaged so badly it had to be torn down and rebuilt, the bowl of strawberries was still sitting where they had left it, with not a berry spilled.

There were, as is always the case with tornadoes, many amazing stories of survival. The tornado picked up one man and carried him for several blocks before it dropped him. He was badly injured, but survived for several years after that. A piece of a 2 x 4 had been driven between his shoulder blades. For the rest of his life, doctors had to pick glass, etc. out of his skin. When he died several years later, it wasn't from injuries sustained in the tornado, but from lung cancer. He had been a heavy smoker for many years.

The storm caught the family of the Pentecostal Church pastor off guard. He and his wife had several children, and the family was happy to find them all relatively unscathed after the tornado passed, except for the two-year-old boy who had disappeared. Word was quickly spread among survivors and a frantic search was started. Soon one of the searchers discovered the boy in the "malarial ditch" which was about 100 yards behind the house. (The malarial ditch is a long, stone-lined ditch built through town many years ago to help drain water that might harbor mosquitoes, which carry malaria.) The little guy was up to his neck in water, and injured severely, but he was alive, and recovered.

The pastor of the First Baptist Church (Ron Lewis) was at home with his baby daughter when he heard the tornado coming. He took the baby and went into the church building next door because the church was built of sturdier materials than the parsonage. He crawled under a bed in the church nursery and covered the baby with his body. The church and the parsonage were destroyed, but the pastor and the baby survived with little or no injury.

Although there were several people killed, those surviving

felt blessed to be alive. Every day for many days the news carried names of those who had died in the past few hours from injuries sustained in the tornado. One strange incident involved a man named Dorsey Jennings, which is not a very common name. My brother was working with a man whose father was Jennings Dorsey, which is also not a common name. When the radio announced that Dorsey Jennings had died as a result of the storm, the man whose father was Jennings Dorsey became hysterical. My brother hurriedly reminded the man that the names were not listed alphabetically by the last name. His father was fine.

Just a year earlier, to the day, a tornado had hit Wilburton, which is 40-something miles west of Heavener. Some of our local young people were attending college in Wilburton, as had Clem a few years earlier. Although many of the downtown businesses were destroyed, none of our local people perished there, although there were 10 or more who died in that tornado. There were also tornadoes that hit several other cities in Oklahoma, some on the 4th and some on the 5th.

After the May 5th tornado in Howe, that date became known as Tornado Day in our area, and residents always stay alert to weather reports on that day. Of course any time there are storms predicted for our area, regardless of the time of year, we are always aware that a tornado could come calling.

Although spring and fall are the times when tornadoes are most common, Heavener was hit a glancing blow by a tornado one year on Christmas Eve. It apparently went over the town, not quite touching down, but causing much damage. The two-story house where Fred Muse and his wife lived was said to be shaking as if ready to blow away, when a huge tree was blown down on it. The tree apparently held it down till the tornado went on over. A woman was killed a mile or so from that house when a large limb was broken off and fell on her as she was running from her car to a friend's storm shelter. She was the only fatality.

In this part of the country, few houses have been built with basements in recent years. This is due to the water table being so near the surface, which makes it very difficult to keep water out of basements or cellars. But many new houses built on higher elevations are now being built with basements to serve as protection from tornadoes.

Many people are having "safe rooms" installed when they build a house, or have storm cellars, which are usually small concrete or metal "boxes" set underground. Ours is about six by six-feet-square, and is placed a few steps from our garage door. While we seldom go in it, we try to keep it ready during storm season, in case we feel a need to go in it.

Living through an experience as we did, where friends and acquaintances lost their lives in a tornado, will cause the bravest soul to make every effort to avoid becoming the victim of one.

Incident in an Art shop

In Honolulu celebrating our silver wedding anniversary, we were walking down the street just to see what was there. We didn't see much that interested us, but walked by an art shop and for some unknown reason, decided to go in and see what they had. It was mostly paintings. They may have been very good paintings. They should have been, according to the prices. But neither of us is a very good judge of art. As far as I'm concerned, there are local people here who paint as well as some of the famous artists, and to me the best art work is that done by grandkids. But we didn't point that out to the saleslady who accosted us the minute we walked through the door. I'm sure she was sizing us up to see if she thought we'd be able to afford any of the overpriced doodling hanging on the walls of the store.

She asked where we were from and we said Oklahoma. Her next question was, "Are you farmers?" I don't know if she was going by our redneck look or if she just thought everyone in Oklahoma farmed. Not that there's a thing wrong with being a farmer. Our parents were farmers and I'm only sorry they had to quit farming before I was born. But they had to make a living and couldn't do that farming. Somehow, the question, or the way she asked it, or just her haughty attitude didn't set well with me. Before I had time to even think about it, I blurted out, "No, he works for the government and I own a business." Which was true. He had been a government employee for many years by then—delivering the U.S. mail. I had a cake business, and on a really good day after a trip to Walmart, I might have as much as five or six hundred dollars in equipment and supplies on hand. If you counted the stove I baked the cakes in and the small AC in the window of my little cake shop behind our house, it would be even more than that. And I had paid for every bit of it with money I had earned myself. Without farming.

All my life I've been nothing but a redneck from the hills of eastern Oklahoma, and have never had any desire to be anything different from that. We've been blessed to travel a lot in the past, but still I hate big cities and can't stand crowds. I've never liked society trying to tell me how to dress, how to act, or what to do with my "leisure time." I couldn't care less what the people around me think I should do or not do. Famous actors or singers are just someone who had a streak of good luck and I don't envy them a bit or have any desire to meet them. I've tried my best to live as the Lord would have me to, often failed, but am still trying. And now I had let an uppity woman derail my best intentions. I had started down a slippery slope of semi-deceit, and I had to try to stay on it just long enough to get out of that store.

Her next question was, "Do you own any Woods?" I can only assume that somebody named Woods has had some success as an artist, but I'm not acquainted with the person. I had to think very carefully what to say, because my first instinct was to say, "Well, we have a few trees out in the pasture, but I'm not sure they would qualify as woods."

But I managed to hold that in and said simply, "Not yet."

I can't remember much more about that incident other than trying to make as hasty and dignified an exit as possible.

As Popeye says, "I yam what I yam and that's all what I am." And there's no need to try to be anything different from that.

Tent Camping

When our kids were growing up, we used to camp a lot. Clem had set a goal of taking our kids to every state in the Union before they left home, and we did accomplish that. But it wasn't easy. The only way Clem could afford to feed his passion for traveling was by doing it the gypsy way—sleeping in a tent and eating what we took with us.

Tent camping was never something I cared for much. In the first place, it virtually always rained when we slept in a tent. That caused Clem a lot of worry as well, because he was always afraid the tent would mildew if we folded it up wet, yet he didn't want to stay put long enough for it to dry out.

Besides that, the tent leaked. And I worried about not having a lock on the door. People used to laugh at me because I would tie a cord from both of my kids' sleeping bags to mine. That way if anybody tried to kidnap them, I would be sure to wake up.

A while back I saw a news program on television about kids who were literally stolen from their families' tents while the parents slept. In at least one case, the kidnapper slit the tent in the back, where the child was sleeping, and stole her away without waking a soul. So see? My concern was justified.

Sometimes, in places like Yellowstone Park where bears were often seen, the four of us would sleep in the station wagon we had at the time. You really have to be friendly to sleep in quarters that close.

One time my brother and his family tent camped with us in a primitive area near Broken Bow. All night, armadillos scratched on the tent and rooted around the edges. After hours of that, I finally dozed off, only to be jarred awake by stomping and moaning outside the tent. My brother, who was notorious for having cramps, was having them on the inside of both thighs. He had staggered outside, trying to keep from disturbing the rest of us, and was trying unsuccessfully to walk off the cramps.

Two Labor Day weekends in a row we met Clem's sister and brother-in-law at Lake Eufaula to camp. The first trip, all six of us were sleeping on cots in our tent. It stormed that night, and lying on the metal cots, we could literally feel the thunder vibrate our rib cages. The tent leaked where the straps that held the poles were attached. But we toughed it out.

The next day, most of the campers in the area left. We thought they were being ridiculous. Locking the barn door after the horse is stolen. We had come to camp and camp we would.

That night it stormed again. There were 85-mile-an-hour winds. We were all up holding on to the tent poles, trying to keep it from blowing down, with water dripping in our faces and running down our necks. Eventually we decided to let go and make a run for it.

We dashed to the two vehicles, which were loaded with food supplies, extra clothing, etc. We all just squeezed in where we could and tried to get a little sleep.

When there was a lull in the storm, Clem went out and took apart the tent, which was flat on the ground by then. There were nine sections of the poles broken. He folded up the tent and lashed it to a concrete picnic table. Then it stormed some more, with even stronger winds.

The next morning, after the storm, we crawled out of the vehicles to assess the damage. I had made a birthday cake for Clem's sister and brought it along. As luck would have it, I had unknowingly slept on the cake. Fortunately, it wasn't a rocky road cake.

The next year we tried it again. This time we set up the tent and hoped to sleep in it, as it was cooler than the pickup campers each family had acquired since the previous year. But at least we had an option if we had to leave the tent.

It rained again, so we wound up crammed into the pickup campers. Ours was tiny and not intended for four people to sleep in. Jim got claustrophobia and threw up.

We decided not to try it again the next year.

There used to be a standing joke in our family that if we needed rain, all they had to do was send us camping. One time we left Heavener with it raining and traveled for three weeks. It rained on us everywhere we went. In one place out west, they said they hadn't had a drop of rain in nine months. Fortunately for them, we arrived just in time. We set up our tent, crawled into our sleeping bags, and it rained.

Every time we called home we heard the same story. "We haven't had a drop of rain since you left." When we drove back into town, it started raining.

In 2003, our old tent long since gone and forgotten, and the kids grown up and gone, we decided to buy a small tent to take on a driving trip to Nova Scotia. We knew it would not be a comfortable way to sleep, but Clem had learned that there are limited accommodations in Nova Scotia and on Prince Edward Island, and he was afraid there might be some nights we would be thankful to have a tent.

We decided to set the tent up in our back yard and try it out before we left on the trip. We hadn't had rain in ages and none was forecast, so when we set up the tent we discussed leaving off the rain fly. I insisted on putting it on, "just to be sure we know how to use it."

During the night we woke up to the pleasant sound of rain on the roof.

We used the tent four nights in Nova Scotia and then gave it away.

Just Another Crazy Day

(I wrote this while HOL (Heavener On Line) was an active blog site, and a while before Clem retired the last time. Craig Hall brought us lots of enjoyment by setting up that blog site and keeping it going. Now he owns and is running the Heavener Ledger more successfully than anyone I can remember in my lifetime. I'm happy for Craig. He's a good man. Things have really slowed down for us now, but it's good to remember.)

Today so far has been one of those weird days when you find yourself holding your breath wondering what's going to happen next.

When we got up this morning, we didn't exactly have any definite plans for the day. I guess it's a good thing.

We were eating a late breakfast when I saw out of the breakfast room window that one of our neighbors across the street was trying to pull a dead tree down with his pickup. It wasn't working. I kept expecting to see the back end of the truck fall out.

Clem has helped the man cut or cut up dead trees before. He's always happy to help, but is hesitant to offer help for fear of appearing to be butting into somebody's business. I asked him if he wanted me to call the neighbor's house and ask if he needed some help. He said that would be fine.

So I called and the man's wife said she thought he was doing okay, but she would ask him. In a minute she called back and said he would appreciate the help, as his chain saw wasn't working so well right now and the tree wasn't coming down otherwise.

So Clem cranked up his saw and went across the street and in a few minutes I heard what I thought were two saws going. Shortly afterwards I saw Clem hurrying down through the trees. The gas cap on his saw had come off and he was soaked with gasoline. He came in and washed up and changed clothes and went back. In a few minutes he was back home and said another neighbor had also brought his saw over to help, so between the three of them, they had made short order of the tree.

We discussed that it seems a shame that neighbors don't take time to just get together and visit like they used to. We shouldn't wait for a need to arise before we get together.

By this time Clem's back was really hurting and I felt especially bad because I had temporarily forgotten that he had been having a lot of back trouble and had volunteered him to do a job he isn't used to doing every day. I tried to get him to go to bed, but he said he still needed to mow the lawn and wanted to get it done before he crashed.

During most of this time I was getting phone calls for various reasons. I would be on the cell and the other one would ring and vice versa. If I had remembered what I forgot, I would have lost it again.

Finally I remembered that I had forgotten to buy two birthday cards that needed to be mailed today, so I went to Dollar General, bought the cards, addressed and stamped them, and tried to get to the Post Office. Of course all three crossings were blocked by a train.

I got tired of running back and forth as the train pulled up and backed up, so I drove up to the crossing by the chicken plant and finally got across. Went to the Post Office and then had to wait on the train again when I started home.

As I was leaving the Post Office, I heard sirens, but didn't think a lot about it till I turned onto the Wister Lake road, where I had to stop for a fire truck to pull out of the station. I thought about following it for a while to see where it was going, but thought better of it. Then I realized it was turning onto Timber Ridge. That really got my attention. I kept looking for smoke as I drove, then realized the fire truck was stopping almost in front of our house.

I remembered Clem had been mowing so for a minute I was afraid something had happened to him.

A crowd was gathered in front of the house where Clem had helped cut the tree earlier, and finally I saw a car in the ditch in front of the house. It had obviously been wrecked, but I couldn't spot a second vehicle. As more of the neighbors gathered, I thought again that it was a shame we had to have an excuse to get together.

I pulled into our driveway and called Clem on the cell to see if he was aware of what was going on out front. He was just getting ready to go hunt me because I had been gone for a while and he was hearing lots of sirens.

We don't know the lady who had the accident. We know where she lives, but haven't met her. She had taken out three mailboxes and hit a tree, and had apparently rolled the car somewhere in the process. She appeared not to be too seriously hurt, but was tightly pinned in the car. We watched as our wonderful firemen used the Jaws of Life to cut that car apart like a tin can. They worked as gently as possible to avoid causing any further injury or alarm to the lady. Heavener is indeed blessed to have such wonderful firemen.

We don't know what caused the accident. The driver told the policeman that she had been having trouble holding the car in the road, and someone who had been following her for miles agreed with that. We wondered if she had had a health problem or a mechanical problem with the car. She was within two or three blocks of home when the accident occurred.

And that brought up the fact again that while Clem has driven in all fifty states, most of them several times, and most of Canada without having so much as a fender bender, he has been involved in several minor accidents near home. In the last one, he had three ribs broken. Yet we tend to worry about our friends and loved ones when they leave on long trips, while it's more likely they'll get hurt right here in town.

So often people walk along this road, or ride bicycles, or children or puppies are in the road. Clem observed that if the Lord didn't watch out for us, something like that accident could occur while some of us were in the way.

I walked back down the driveway after the ambulance left with the lady, and noticed that the waterfall in the B's park wasn't on, and stopped to investigate. It wasn't working, so I pulled it out and turned it over to poor Clem, whose back was really hurting by now. He finally had to give up on it and go in to rest.

My brother arrived shortly before then to borrow something, but didn't stay long.

It's almost four and I still don't have the breakfast dishes washed. Now I remember why we usually just run around on Saturday.

Written around 2009.

Cleaning Out the Attic

Anytime I mention buying something, my husband will say, "It's fine to buy it. But where are you going to put it?" I'll admit that in 50 years of marriage we've collected a lot of, well, junk. Much of it came from his parents, and mine. None of that stuff would be worth a nickel if we tried to sell it, but there's always sentiment to consider.

Now I'm not one of those women who thinks every square inch of wall space has to be covered with something colorful. You can actually see the dust on the top of most of our furniture, while some of my friends have so much stuff on theirs that you couldn't find a place to put down a toothpick.

But we both, like most people our age, do have some things we've kept for sentimental value, and they tend to accumulate. We kept things for years thinking our kids would have a use for them someday. But they don't want the old wooden potty chair, high chair, or their first bicycle. Their old toys are just so much trash to them. We both have our old bicycles, dating from the 40's and 50's, stashed far back in the attic of our storage building. We can't throw them out, because they have sentimental value for us. I guess the younger generation just isn't sentimental.

We also have everything left from my husband's parents that his siblings left behind after picking over their parents' belongings and taking what they wanted. And my husband can't stand to throw the stuff out.

For the life of me, I can't imagine how you can be sentimental about old rusty chains, plow points, and other equally worthless landfill that my husband's dear old dad left behind. I loved him, too, but I can't see where it would be at all disrespectful to throw out most of that junk.

On the other hand, I have a lot of old dishes from both his mother and mine. The bulk of them are cracked and chipped, and one of these days I'm going to toss them out. But for now, those worthless dishes are taking up space in the attic. The rest of them, some perhaps slightly saleable on the merits of being unchipped and uncracked and quite old, might be worth a few dollars, sentiment aside.

Unfortunately, through the years since his parents died in 1973, and mine in the 90's, I've forgotten from which mother any particular dish came. So much for sentiment.

We have most of a closet filled with old computer paraphernalia. I can't throw it out because I don't know what's worth anything, and he won't throw it out for fear he might need it again. There's even a roll of paper from an ancient fax machine. Anyone want it?

I have really nice clothes dating back to the 70's that I hate to part with, because I keep hoping that one day I might lose enough weight to get back into them. The fact that they would be totally out of style now bothers me very little. I found some old dresses of mine in the attic, kept for sentimental reasons, such as those my mother made for me. Now I might get one leg in them in the space where my body used to fit. But I can look at them and see my mother bent over the old sewing machine, lovingly sewing every stitch. Trashing them would seem like trashing my mother.

I also have my dad's favorite purple shirt, as well as some of his patched overalls and a tattered jacket he used to wear while working outside. I can almost smell the oil and gasoline on them from when he wore them while working on lawn mowers. Too bad I had to launder them, as they have lost the lingering scent of my hard-working dad. Looking at them brings to mind my dad's gnarled old hands, with black grease imbedded in the skin and under the nails, evidence that he had worked well past his ability to do so, scratching out another dollar to take care of those he loved.

A sampling of my husband's old Post Office uniforms fills up another box. When he retired, they gave him the old leather mail bag he had used when he first went to work for the Post Office in 1957. At least they know how to dispose of stuff they no longer use.

I have more books than some small-town libraries. Most of them came from sales of one kind or another, or from the 10-cent box of old volumes at the local library. I thought that once I got old and feeble and unable to do anything else, I might have time to read them. It never occurred to me that my eyes might go along with or even before the rest of my body.

And besides all that, I don't need but three books. By the time I've read the last one of the three, I've forgotten what the first one said, so I can start all over.

So a while back, I decided to start culling the books. I threw out about four of them that I knew were totally outdated and would never be needed again. I also bagged up a few to try to give them away. Somehow that bag wound up in the back of the truck with things we both agreed we could stand to part with.

The next day I found that bag back in the house. My husband

explained that he felt sure I would like to keep the books. I never would have missed them.

Last week I decided that the time had come that I must clean out the attic. I don't want to die and leave the mess for the kids to have to go through, although I think it would be easier for them to do than it is for me. Nothing there is worth a cent to them and they could chuck it all out and laugh while doing it.

The attic had become so cluttered and crowded that it was unsafe to set foot up there. My husband cheered as I tossed box after box and bag after bag off the upper deck and near the truck, to be hauled off. Some of the boxes and bags actually had something in them. It was mostly stuff that had so deteriorated in the heat of the attic that it fell apart when picked up.

I have had an old doll since I was five years old, and it has been virtually dead and decomposed for at least 40 years. But to me, throwing out a doll or photos of people borders on voodoo.

While cleaning the attic, I found that doll again, carefully packed away in a box and wrapped in an old scarf. I took it out and looked at it carefully. The cloth body has long since been reduced to shreds. The legs and arms hang by a thread. The head, legs, and arms are made of some kind of fiber, and covered with perhaps some early kind of plastic, known back then as "celluloid" and pronounced "sittleoid" by most people I ever heard try to pronounce it.

The extremities all look like they had been severely sunburned, with the skin peeling off in huge clumps. The poor thing was just so sad to look at that I decided the time had come when I must be strong and just let it go. I should have gone out back, dug a deep hole, and given it a decent burial. But I didn't really have time to do that, and besides, there was snow on the ground. So I carried it down, in its box, and carefully placed it on top of the other trash in the back of the truck.

The next day before he hauled the stuff away, my husband told me very gently that he had something to ask me. He said, "I see you've thrown your doll away, and I wonder if you really want to do that. I'm afraid you might be sorry later and wish you hadn't done it."

So I told him to set it aside and I'd take it back to the attic.

I give up. We both want things culled out, but neither of us has what it takes to do it. If the kids don't want our house enough to go to the trouble of sorting through our stuff, they can just say so and we'll leave it to someone who loves junk more than we do.

Why I Like my Kids

As with most folks, our two kids, Sandy and Jim, have been the brightest spot in our lives. They were both very good kids. Never once did either of them get in trouble with the law or get in trouble at school. We always told the kids that if they got a ticket for some driving offense, they would find a way to pay it. We would never bail them out of any trouble they got themselves into.

As I recall, the nearest they ever came to it, was when Jim got stopped for speeding on his way to the bowling alley at Poteau when he was in college at Carl Albert. He had three of his friends with him, and they were running late because one of them had been late getting to our house. In trying to get to the bowling alley and get checked in before the rates changed, he was driving a little too fast. And of course he got stopped and ticketed.

The officer asked him what his hurry was and he told him frankly that he was trying to get to the bowling alley before the rates changed for the night. Afterwards, one of his friends told him that he should have been able to come up with a better story than that. Jim told him he wasn't going to lie about it.

The first thing he did was to sell his "fuzz buster" which he had bought with money he had earned working at the IGA. He planned to use that money to pay his fine. When he went to see the official he was to report to, he turned out to be someone who knew Clem's family. Clem had grown up with that official's mother. So he wanted to discuss Clem's flying and other things they had in common. At the end of the conversation with Jim tied up in knots waiting to hear the worst, he told Jim, "You're allowed one speeding ticket in five years." So he had sold his fuzz buster for nothing. Come to think of it, it must not have worked very well anyway.

One of our older friends used to say, "Every old crow thinks her little one is the blackest," and we were no exception. Our kids are not perfect, but we think they come pretty close to it. One thing about them that makes me happy is the way they love each other and help each other in any way possible. When Jim's house flooded a few years ago, Sandy and her husband Steve went down and helped shovel the mud out and helped any way they could. Sandy has talked about how, when they were small, if someone gave Jim something, such as a piece of candy, he always asked if he could have one for his sister. I never knew them to fight over anything, except, as Sandy always insisted, when Jim started pestering her and wouldn't stop. When the subject is brought up even now, after 40 years, Sandy always insists, "Jim always started it."

One of the worst things we've been through with our kids was when Sandy had breast cancer in 2009. She had a double mastectomy and endured all the pain and sickness involved in chemo treatment. Literally for years. And when Jim spent 13 days in the hospital at Fort Smith, AR, in traction, after having a hip dislocated in a casual game of football with some of his friends on a Sunday afternoon. And when he was bitten by a copperhead...

Thankfully, Sandy is still doing well eleven years later. Jim had to have that hip replaced a few years ago and has had multiple surgeries involving his shoulders, arms, and hands. But they are strong and God is good.

Deaf as a What?

One of the most frustrating things about growing old is losing your hearing. If you can't laugh at yourself, you're in trouble.

So I'm in the kitchen and Clem is looking at his iPhone in the living room. He says, "Jane Doe posted that she has blackberries in her back yard."

Me: "Jane Poe?"

Clem: "No, Jane Loe."

Me: "Jane Loe?"

Clem: Shouting. "NO!!!!!JANE DOE!"

So I walk into the living room and say, "So why did she post it? Does she want someone to come and pick them?"

No reply.

Me. Very loud. "SO DOES SHE WANT YOU TO COME AND PICK THEM?"

Clem: "Pick what?"

Me: "The blackberries."

Clem: "What blackberries?"

Me: "The ones you said Jane Poe has in her back yard."

Pause.
Clem: "I didn't say black BERRIES. I said black BEAR!"
Don't blame it on me. I'd get a hearing aid if he would.

Grandkids

Sandy taught her first child, Cara, to read at the age of four. When they were driving in the car, she'd sit and rehearse her phonics.

After having a bout with the stomach flu, they heard her working on her letters again. A, Ay, Ate; B, Buh, Ball; C, Cuh, Cat; D, Duh, Diarrhea.

Cara turned two on November 1st and when they came to the house for Thanksgiving, she was ready to help with everything. I was trying to make a meatloaf one day and she was up there with her hands in the meat, working away. I started to salt the meat and for some reason, I salted her hands as well. She just shook the salt off and said, "Mamaw's c'azy!" I mentioned it at the table that night and someone didn't believe she had said that, at barely two years old, and said so. Cara shrugged her little shoulders and said, "Mamaw IS c'azy!" And now that they're all grown up with little ones of their own, I'm still known as the c'azy Mamaw.

* * *

We were eating in a restaurant with our 2 ½ year-old granddaughter,

Camden, and her family when a baby at a nearby table pulled a glass of water off the table, spilling it on herself. Her mother moved her from the high chair and set her in the booth beside her, while she cleaned up the spill. I was watching to see what the baby was going to do when Camden said, "Don't look at her, Mamaw. She's in time out."

* * *

When Jim's daughter, Aspen, was two, we were visiting them, and I went into the bedroom to get my curling iron. Aspen followed me in there, climbed up on the bed, and sat there with her feet crossed as she watched me.

"Whatcha doin', Mamaw?"

"I just came in to get my curling iron."

"How tum?"

"I need to fix my hair."

"How tum? Your hair bwoke?"

* * *

Shortly before Christmas, my husband was reading our then-two-year-old granddaughter, Autumn, her favorite book. He would read, "The pretty birds sing a song for you. Who made the birds?"

Having heard the story many times before, Autumn would answer enthusiastically, "Dod did!"

The story went on to name many other animals, ask who made them, and Autumn was always ready with the same answer.

That night we were driving through Honor Heights Park in Muskogee looking at the beautiful Christmas lights. Among the other displays were a number of animal outlines filled and covered with lights. Autumn was fascinated. Eventually she sighed contentedly and said quietly, almost to herself, "You know, Dod sure is nice sometimes."

Mary and Jophus

At Christmas time, when all the kids and grands were home, the two youngest granddaughters were off in a bedroom playing with dolls. After a while, they came through the living room, both wearing baby blankets as scarves over their heads and wrapped around their shoulders. Autumn, four, was carrying a doll, also wrapped in a blanket, and Camden, three, was walking very carefully beside her. Someone asked them what they were doing. Autumn explained that the doll was baby Jesus and she was Mary. And Camden added, "And I'm Jophus." I never hear of a Joe or Joseph that I don't think of Jophus and Mary.

The Hills

Clem grew up at Howe and for a number of years we belonged to Howe Faith Baptist Church. It was a wonderful time and we made some great friends there.

One family who was and is special to us was the Hills. They have three kids, Bradley, Bentley, and Cammie. Brad and Bentley fell in between Sandy and Jim, age-wise, and Cammie was about Jim's age. I always loved it when the two families got together.

The Hills live in the country and keep some livestock. They also make a huge garden every year, and Jeannie is hands-down the best cook I've ever known.

Jeannie was a stay-at-home mom like me, but when Cammie started to school, Jeannie started to college and became a teacher. She is one of the most giving, loving people I've ever known. At one point, the church received a letter from an older lady in the area, thanking the church for providing her with a hot-water heater and having it installed for her. No one seemed to know anything about it. Upon investigation, we learned that Jeannie had gone to visit the woman, had seen her need, and had provided the water heater in the church's name. Seems she used part of a grant or loan given to help her with college expenses. She graduated from college and taught for a number of years at Monroe.

Brad also grew up and became a teacher and a minister, and for a while was in administration at the school at Monroe. Bentley has been Baptist Student Union director at Carl Albert State College for a number of years, and the last I knew Cammie had been working for the school at Howe for years. Truman and Jeannie now keep two or three great-grandchildren for three days a week while their parents work. They both retired years ago, Jeannie from teaching and Truman from the Department of Human Services.

Truman once told us about an incident involving a man who was drawing a check from the Department of Human Services. He mentioned no name, of course. Truman had made a routine call to the man's house and the man saw him coming. I suppose, knowing that Truman had a good sense of humor, he decided to play a prank on him. When Truman knocked on the door, the man opened the door and shoved a gun in his stomach, saying, "I'll teach you to cut off my check!" He had the gun loaded with blanks and actually pulled the trigger. Suffice it to say that Truman was not amused by that prank.

After the kids were all grown and married, I had occasion to call Cammie for something one day, but kept getting a wrong number. I thought. I finally called her mother-in-law to ask if they had had their number changed. She said no, but she thought Truman was at their house that day. I called the number again and got the same answer as before, "Joe's bar and grill." It was Truman, of course. I should have recognized his voice the first time. I always loved to hear him laugh. And he had enjoyed getting a good one on me.

One interesting thing about the Hills involves their house. When she finished high school, Jeannie went off to Oklahoma City to work, and was to come back early in May, when she and Truman would be wed in the First Baptist church at Howe. On May 5th, 1961, a tornado hit Howe, killed numerous people, and destroyed much of the town, including the First Baptist church building. A few miles north of Howe is the small community called Number 10, and the old school house was still standing. So they hurriedly got the place cleaned up and had their wedding there. Faith Baptist church was also established there and remained there till a new building could be built in Howe. A few years down the road, Truman and Jeannie bought that #10 building and turned it into a lovely house, where they still live. Incidentally, they built a storm cellar under their bedroom, accessed by a trap door a few feet from their bed. Seeing what a tornado can do changes a person's view on storms.

The Hornbacks

Oral and Louise Hornback were also good friends at Faith. Oral died fairly young after suffering from Parkinson's for many years. Their daughter, Linda, married Joe Haydon Hall, who was our first pastor at Faith, and she taught school for many years. Really good people.

Their other daughters were Cheryl, who, although handicapped, is one of the sweetest people I ever met. As far as I know, she's still living in the Oaks Nursing Home at Poteau. Kelli was the youngest daughter and so sweet and kind. She became a nurse and has worked as one for many years now.

Louise used to call me on the phone occasionally and we'd talk for a long time. Maybe not for hours, but it seemed like it. I loved to hear her laugh and she laughed a lot. It always gave me a lift to visit with her. The strange thing about Louise was that she chased rabbits, but she always made it back to the subject at hand. We could be talking about some subject, which would remind her of something else, and off she'd go. But, unlike me, she would eventually get back to the first subject. Not me. If I ever ran off after a rabbit I never made it back to whatever we had been talking about before. I always loved visiting with her, but her calls came less and less often and eventually she could no longer keep up with the rabbits either. She was about 10 years my senior, and she passed away a few years ago. I still miss her.

The Cat That Changed My Mind

When I was growing up, I always had a cat. I never had one that was purely a house cat, so they never lived very long. Either they got run over in the street or another bigger cat or neighborhood dogs killed them, or they just died or disappeared. I was always heartbroken, but before long another one would come along and help me heal.As a preschooler, I wore cats around my neck for a fur stole, put them in my doll bed and pretended they were babies, dressed them up in doll clothes, and confided in them when trouble came along. Cats were often the best friends I had.

When our daughter was small, a stray kitten came along and she adopted it. She carried it around upside and it didn't seem to mind. Back then it never occurred to us to have cats vaccinated as we did dogs. It's a wonder none of us was ever bitten by a cat and forced to have rabies shots. One day we drove up in the driveway just in time to see the kitten having a fit. Needless to say, the kitten had to be put down.

My father-in-law who lived behind us always had some cats, and the kittens would find their way to our house. Jim had arrived by then, and from the start was as much a cat person as I was.

Only he loved dogs just as much or more. Each time Pap had a new batch of kittens, Sandy and Jim each picked out one they considered their pets. Sandy's always disappeared before long. I don't know if it was the fact that hers always disappeared before long, or what happened to her, but she soon lost her love for cats.

One summer when Sandy was about thirteen, my cousin's eleven-year-old daughter came from Indiana to visit us. She stayed for several weeks. Horrible weeks. The night we arrived home from Indiana, Amy played with my parents' neighbor's cat. The cat bit her on the finger. The next morning the cat was found dead on my parents' back porch. When we asked the neighbors if the cat had been vaccinated for rabies, they weren't sure.

That day was a holiday, probably July 4th, and all government offices were closed. I knew the man who was head of the Health Department in Poteau, so started trying to call him.

When we finally located him, he said to bring the cat's head to the Health Department to be tested for rabies. Finally he said just bring the cat in and he would take care of it.

My husband took the cat up there and the man explained how to remove the head if such a thing should happen again. Needless to say, we spent a few tense days waiting for the results. We discussed calling Amy's mother, but knew she would worry and would not be able to come for a few weeks, so we just dealt with it as we would have if it had been one of our own who was bitten

At that time, my father-in-law's old cat had a litter of young kittens. Amy was such a cat lover that she couldn't keep her hands off them. A few days after the first incident, she picked up a kitten to pet. Our dog rushed up to investigate, the kitten panicked, bit Amy through the thumb, jumped from her arms, ran under the playhouse, and died. Needless to say, we were horrified. Here was the same situation again.

The man at the Health Department had told Clem that a dead animal suspected of being rabid should be handled only with rubber gloves. As I was the only one who had rubber gloves (too small for Clem) it fell my lot to remove the kitten's head. It was one of the hardest things I ever did in my life. Amy cried and said, "How can you stand to do that?" I told her I couldn't, that I did it for her sake, because it had to be done.

So here we were, waiting for the report to come back on the second kitten when we still hadn't received the report on the first. Meanwhile, I took Amy to be checked over, and was told she needed a tetanus shot. I really hated to do it, but as she was unsure when she had had a tetanus shot and didn't want her mother called, we went ahead and had the shot.

Thankfully, the report on both cats showed they had died of feline distemper and they did not have rabies. Then more fun began. The rest of the kittens started dropping like flies. The only cats to survive were an old tom that had come to us years before, and my father-in-law's old female. We learned that older cats seem to be more or less immune to feline distemper.

Suddenly I realized that a drastic change had come over me. I no longer wanted to go anywhere near a cat. I didn't even want to see one.

One night months later, we were at a relative's house, and young kittens were running around on the porch, where we were sitting visiting. The sight of the kittens made me literally shudder. They looked like rats to me.

For several years, I wanted nothing whatsoever to do with cats.

Then one day my neighbor Betty and I were taking our usual morning walk from her house up towards the Morris Creek Road to the Morris Creek Bridge, down the road that connected the Morris Creek Road to the Old Pike, and down the Pike back to her house. As we were finishing our walk, a scrawny black kitten came running from an isolated barn to meet us.

I shuddered at the sight, picked up an empty can from the ditch, and threw it at him. "Shoo! Go back! You can't go home with me. My dog would eat you," I yelled at the kitten. It went back, but the next morning it was at our house. Our dog seemed to ignore it.

My husband told me and the kids not to feed the kitten and maybe it would go away. It didn't. Maybe because the dog shared his food with it. Or maybe because some other anonymous people felt sorry for it and fed it. In any case, the kitten stayed.

Jim's old dog was about 15 years old by then, and spent most of the time sleeping. So Jim started petting the kitten. One night he called us into his room after he had gone to bed. The kitten was on the brick section outside and just below his high window, looking in at him and purring like crazy.

One day I was stripping the old varnish from a piece of furniture out on the back walk. The kitten chased the brush I was using and got the paint remover on his paws. I picked him up and washed his paws with water from the garden hose. He purred the whole time. By the time it had happened four or five times, I realized I had some good feelings for the kitten. What a trooper he was! And what a sweet nature he had.

To shorten the story a lot, I will just say that that scrawny black kitten who became Ebony, stayed at our house for 16 years. Even my husband, who has never been a cat lover, came to love that cat. He was a rare find. He was the only cat we've ever owned who was allowed to stay in the house, as he never offered to jump up on a table or cabinet and never bothered anything.

I think God sent Eb to me to help me learn to love cats again.

The night Eb died, not unexpectedly, he had gone to his litter box, crawled in, and died peacefully. We buried him just as we found him. Even in death, he had gone out of his way not to be a bother. How could anybody not love a cat like that?

Epilogue

One of the most popular places to walk in Heavener is the Heavener Memorial Park Cemetery. Clem walks there fairly often. I walk there occasionally. It's really hard for me to get any walking done up there, because I find myself constantly stopping to visit with friends and loved ones who have made that their final resting place. All of my immediate birth family, with the exception of one, are buried there. Clem has a grandfather buried there, but most of his relatives are buried elsewhere.

I see the markers for so many loved ones, friends, and neighbors from the past, bringing good memories of their love and kindness. I find myself rejoicing that most of them are in Heaven, maybe looking down and cheering this wobbly old lady on to get in just a few more steps. We walk by and check on the lots that will be our final resting place. I see them as a joyful place to wind up. It seems good to me to think that we'll be placed near people we knew growing up. I look at the marker for Buck Olive and almost laugh out loud. We'll be spending time with him as our next-door neighbor when our time walking on the streets of Heavener is up. Buck was such a jolly man and when I used to go in Olive Bros.

grocery as a child, he always gave me a hard time. His name for me was Patrick. I can still see him in his butcher's apron, behind the meat counter, doing his job and cheering up people. I can also see him running down the street, still in his apron, to join the other volunteer firemen to rush to the scene of a fire.

His brother Clyde will also be nearby and I think of Clyde with fondness. He was such a good man, but without the humor that Buck always displayed.

Clem says he probably delivered mail to the homes of at least half the people whose names we see in the cemetery, so walking up there is like old home week.

It seems we have so many more friends and loved ones on the other side than we have still here with us. But that's okay. To be absent from the body is to be present with God. Either way, we are so blessed.

For anyone reading this after we have gone on, I want you to know that if you ever spoke a kind word to me, thought charitably about me, overlooked a fault of mine, said a prayer for me, or if you were good to my family, it meant so much to me. God bless you every one!

About the Author

Patsy (Pat) Linville was born in 1941 to Earl and Adele Linville in Forester, Arkansas, where Earl worked for the Caddo River Lumber Company. When Pat was a month old, they moved to Heavener, OK, where Earl ran an automotive repair business. Pat has always enjoyed writing. As sixth graders, she and her friend,

Alton Manifold, often wrote stories for each other, for entertainment purposes only. Alton grew up and went to work for a big city newspaper, and Pat married Clem Burroughs, her postman, and raised two kids. She had a home-based cake decorating business for many years, also working in local businesses, as a substitute teacher and a volunteer tutor with first graders, and later a church secretary for seven years. Through the years, she has been published in a number of newspapers and magazines. While she never considered writing a book until recent years, friends have often encouraged her to do so. This book is a compilation of short writings saved from many years of "just jotting things down."

CPSIA information can be obtained
at www.ICGtesting.com
Printed in the USA
LVHW091803220121
677210LV00035B/567

9 781950 794409